LA 10/15

ABOUT THE AUTHOR

Siobhan is an awarding-winning author, coach and speaker. She loves daring others to love, create and dream – and show their true face to the world. Her first novel for young adults, *Dear Dylan*, was winner of the Young Minds Book Award and her Shipwrecked series is currently being developed for television. She was also editorial consultant for Zoe Sugg on her novel, *Girl Online*. When Siobhan isn't writing she can usually be found contorted into a weird shape on a yoga mat or at a dance workshop. She can be found online at: www.siobhancurham.co.uk and on Twitter at: @siobhancurham.

For more information about this book and about Siobhan's True Face workshops and talks, please go to: www.TrueFaceRevolution.com

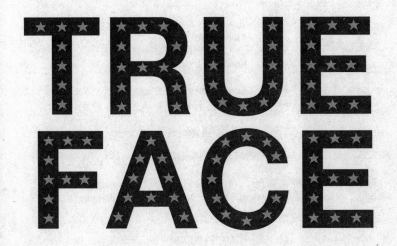

TRUE FACE

Siobhan Curham

FABER & FABER

First published by Faber & Faber Ltd in 2015
Bloomsbury House
74–77 Great Russell Street
London WC1B 3DA

Typeset by Faber & Faber Ltd
Printed and bound by CPI Group (UK) Ltd, Croydon, CRO 4YY

A CIP record for this book
is available from the British Library

ISBN 978-0-571-31338-9

FSC
www.fsc.org
MIX
Paper from
responsible sources
FSC® C101712

2 4 6 8 10 9 7 5 3 1

This book is dedicated to YOU.
May you dream boldly, love fearlessly and live
your truth.

Don't show me your tweet-face
Or ur txt spk
Show me your True Face
And let your heart speak.

♥

CONTENTS

INTRODUCTION

'All the world's a stage, and all the men and women merely players,' wrote William Shakespeare, way back in 1600. It only takes a quick scroll through our Twitter or Facebook feeds to tell us that, despite being centuries old, this quote has never been more relevant.

Today, it can all too often feel as if we are performing our lives in front of a huge audience, and we are inundated with conflicting directions about how we should act. The internet, magazines and media bombard us with images of how thin, sexy and downright perfect we should be (conveniently ignoring the fact that these images are mainly air-brushed illusions). Celebrities endlessly tell us how to live, what to eat and how to love – right before checking into rehab/'fessing up to an eating disorder/ being cheated on by a two-timing love rat. At school and college our teachers demand we make decisions that will affect the rest of our lives, without ever bothering to ask us what we want that life to be. And even though our friends and family have our best interests at heart, they can only ever offer advice based on their own personal viewpoint of the world, not ours.

There is a massive problem at the heart of this way of living: *it isn't real*. When you start letting other people and events dictate how you live your life, you stop being true to yourself. Just as Shakespeare said, you end up becoming a 'mere player' and can end up in situations that leave you feeling empty, unhappy and afraid. But when you take the time to discover who you really are and what you really want, your life story becomes way more exciting than any play or film. And the really great news is, once you are no longer acting a part, you get to become truly authentic.

A truly authentic woman is never afraid to be herself, never apologises for being herself and never settles for second best. She is in full control of her life and never a mere player. She is fascinating, complex, vulnerable, strong, sassy, smart and unique. She is perfectly imperfect. She is *you*.

This book is part mystery, part adventure. The mystery is working out who you truly are, and the adventure comes in planning the kind of life you really want to lead. In the coming chapters, I will help you peel away the ways in which you've been 'performing' and guide you back to your true self. I will share my own personal experiences and those of others who have made the journey back to truth. I was barely able to type some of my personal recollections I was cringing so much! But I wrote them because I've come to realise that you don't get anywhere until you get real. And for you to get the most from this book, you're going to need to get real too.

At the end of each chapter you'll find exercises designed to help you on your personal journey of self-discovery. A lot of these exercises involve writing or jotting down random thoughts, so you might want to get a notebook as a companion to this book – your True Face journal. You can do these exercises as you go along, or you might want to read the book through first, then come back and use the interactive sections as a workshop. Whatever you feel is right for you. Closing each chapter is a power tweet with the TrueFace hashtag. Please feel free to share these if you feel moved to do so. And why not highlight any parts of this book that resonate with you so that you can find them again quickly if you need to. Together we are going to embark upon a wonderful journey of self-discovery. From now on there will be no more, 'Keep Calm and Carry On'. Instead, 'Forget the Fake and Keep it Real' will become our mantra. Ready . . . ?

You don't get anywhere until you get real
#TrueFace

PART ONE

★ ★ ★ ★ ★ ★ ★ ★ ★

True Face

1
WHO ARE YOU?

----------- ★ -----------

*I stopped pretending to myself that I was
anything other than what I was, and began
to direct all my energy into finishing the only
work that mattered to me.*

J. K. Rowling

Who are you?
Who are you, *really*?

- -

If you're like most people, you never really give this question very much thought. The chances are, you're too busy trying to do well, please others and fit in. Sure, you'll be able to answer this question at a surface level – *I'm a daughter/sister/student/friend/girlfriend/employee at Rat Race Incorporated* – but these answers are all 'official' rather than authentic. They're all about your roles and not about *you*.

There's an ancient Zen Buddhist saying that I love: 'Show me your original face, the face you had before your parents were born.'

Basically, the Zen Buddhists believed that before we're physically born, we're all one hundred per cent, genuinely us. There's no falseness, no pretence, we are just our own organic, additive-free selves. But as soon as we grow up, we start faking. We don't mean to, it's just that life can be tough – it can throw things at us that leave us feeling anxious and hurt. Maybe a friend laughs at us, or a parent or teacher criticises something we do. We become scared to show our 'original' face in case we'll be hurt or made to feel stupid again.

So we put on other faces, like masks. This can be an *'I'm so happy'* face, or an *'I don't give a damn'* face, or an *'I'm really tough'* face. But none of them are genuine. And, when we cover our true selves up, we start acting inauthentically too and this can cause major problems. A perfect example of this process in action often takes place, rather aptly, on *Face*book.

The trouble with *Fake*booking

- -

Picture the scene: Amelie is a twenty-something writer. She shares an apartment with her best friend. Recently, Amelie and her boyfriend Jack broke up. They'd been together for several years. He was her first date, her first kiss, her first teenage love, but over the years they have drifted apart and their love drifted into companionship. Although she was really sad at the time of their split, Amelie is proud of how well she has dealt with it since. She has thrown herself into writing her first novel and is spending lots of quality time with her friends.

So, when she wakes up one Monday morning a couple of months after the break-up, she is feeling warm and sleepy and calm. Then she turns on her phone and she logs on to Facebook. As she scrolls through her news feed, she sees a sight that makes her blood freeze. Last night, Jack uploaded a new photo. It is of him sitting in a bar with his arm draped round a girl. As Amelie wipes the sleep from her eyes, she becomes convinced that the girl is gazing at Jack with an expression that can only be described as 'adoring'. Amelie's heart starts racing and she feels sick but, rather than putting the phone down, she looks at the comments below the picture. *Great night*, Jack has written, followed by a smiley face. Never has an emoticon looked so sinister.

Amelie feels tears burning her eyes. She scrolls down to try and distract herself from what she's seen but negative thoughts start clogging her mind.

I can't believe he's met someone already!

I can't believe he would post a picture of them together!

She looks so into him.

She looks so cheap!

Why would he go for someone like her?

I thought he loved me.

He can't have loved me if he's with someone else already.

Maybe he never loved me!

Maybe our whole relationship was a lie?

Then, as Amelie carries on scrolling, she sees a status update from a writer friend. *Can't believe I've got another book deal*, it reads. If Amelie hadn't been reeling from Jack's post she would have felt happy for her friend – she would have posted a comment congratulating her. But because Amelie is now on the down escalator to doom, all she can think are negative thoughts. She's got *another* book deal. Amelie hasn't even had one book deal yet! Maybe she never will. Once again, she becomes consumed with self-doubt.

What if my novel is rubbish?

What if I end up unpublished and single and unloved my entire life?

Amelie feels as if her world is over before her day has even begun. And yet this whole scenario – and the way it has made Amelie feel – is based on an untruth.

What Amelie doesn't know is that Jack actually had a horrendous time last night. Ever since their break-up, he has been moping about, comfort-eating cereal from the pack and playing an endless soundtrack of 'their song', interspersed with angry rap. Last night, his friends staged an intervention and dragged him out to a bar. While he was there he met his friend Joe's cousin Anna from Sweden – the girl in the picture. Anna was bubbly and fun and she had photos taken with everyone in the group. It was her last night in Manchester and Jack will never see her again. He posted the photo because he wants the world to know that he is over Amelie. He wants *Amelie* to know that he is over Amelie. But the truth is, he isn't – and he won't be for a long time. Amelie will now spend the rest of the day, and probably longer, knocked off-kilter and hating the world, and all because Jack was *Fake*booking. That night Amelie will post a *Fake*book update of her own – informing the world – and Jack – that she is *so happy right now.*

But she isn't. And she won't be for a long time. And Jack won't be when he sees it either.

Is any of this ringing any bells for you?

Okay, it's confession time. In the past, I've lied on my Facebook status updates too. Shocking, I know, but I have a feeling that I'm not the only one. You see, there have been times when I've been really hurting about something, but I haven't wanted the rest of the world to know about it, because I don't want the rest of the world to think that I'm weak, or depressing, or an out-and-out loser. So, instead of writing an honest update from my 'True Face', I've written something witty and zany about how my life is just one big FUN-O-RAMA – which, of course, is completely FAKE-O-RAMA. Let me give you a couple of examples:

Fakebook update:
Having such a fun time in Edinburgh! ☺

True Face update:
Having such a sad time in Edinburgh. Keep thinking about the one person I'd come away to try and forget ☹

_Fake_book update:
Really loving my new life in the country! ☺ ☺ ☺

True Face update:
Really missing my London friends and terrified
I've made a massive mistake by moving to a place
where the buses only come twice an hour ☹ ☹ ☹

Faking in the real world

- -

But it's not just when we're online that we lie about
who or how we are – it can be all too tempting to
fake it in the 'real' world too.

IT consultant Rachel had a really tough time during
her school years. Her shyness meant that she found it
hard to make friends and so she drifted along, hanging
out with the other quiet kids but never properly
connecting with any of them. 'I used to really envy the
popular kids,' she says, 'life seemed to be so easy for
them and making friends seemed so effortless.'

When Rachel got a place at a university a long way
from her home in London, she jumped at the chance
to reinvent herself.

'One of the first nights we were there, a group of us were having a drink in the Student Union bar. I thought that this was my big chance, that if I didn't make a good first impression, I'd fade away into the background like I always did. So I told them that my dad owned a pub in London. This couldn't be further from the truth as, in reality, my dad was a librarian. But one of the cool girls in my school had lived in a pub and it had always seemed such an exciting life to me. My new friends did seem impressed when I told them and at first it felt lovely thinking that they actually saw me as this cool, publican's daughter. But it wasn't long before it became a nightmare.

That first Christmas holiday, one of my uni friends was coming down to London and she asked if she could come and visit me at my parents' pub. I had to make up something to get out of it and I hated lying to her again. In the end, I told everyone that my dad had sold the pub. But I still wasn't able to invite any of my uni friends to come and stay with me during holidays, in case they found out. The whole thing was really stressful and when I look back now I can see that it was totally pointless. My friends from uni never liked me because of what they thought my parents did – they liked me for me. I didn't need to lie. The massive irony is that by lying to try and make friends, I was never able to get as close to those friends as I would have wanted. It was a huge relief to leave uni and start over again. I've been completely honest about my background with the friends I've made through work and it's been *so* much easier!'

As Rachel's example shows, life can sometimes put us under extreme pressure to fake it. And we can put ourselves under extreme pressure to fake it. Put simply:

self-doubt + pressure to be accepted = temptation to fake

But what if we were to eliminate self-doubt and accept ourselves fully? Then we would find that:

self-belief + self-acceptance = True Face

In the first part of this book, I'm going to help you to bring this second equation into life. Into *your* life. Step by step, we're going to peel away the layers, until we get back to who you truly are. Then we're going to work together to make you truly proud of that person. And when you feel truly proud of who you are, you'll stop being so concerned about what the rest of the world thinks or expects of you and your True Face will become your default setting.

One of the best ways in which you can start this process is by focusing on your feelings.

How are you?
How are you *really*?

In your journal, write the title, **TrueFace Update –** or **#TrueFace** if you're a tweeter not a Facebooker. Then write an update about yourself and how you're feeling with total True Face sincerity. Don't worry if it goes on for more than 140 characters. Don't worry if it goes on for pages and pages. It's really important not to hold anything back. Let every horrible thought and fear on to the page. Think of this exercise as tipping up a bin and giving it a really good shake; you want every last piece of rubbish to come tumbling out. I know that getting honest like this can feel uncomfortable at first but it also brings a great sense of release. It can be hard work pretending to be something that you're not. Whenever I own up to myself about how I'm really feeling, I always feel a whole lot freer.

Now, I'm not suggesting you actually *do* this on your social networks. Opening up in this way is about getting really honest with yourself. If you know that hundreds of people will be reading what you write it could leave you feewling vulnerable and exposed and this in turn may cause you to hold back. Get into the habit of writing a True Face update every day in your journal and pretty soon you won't feel the need for any phoney online updates. By releasing your negative thoughts and emotions in this safe and private way, you'll start clearing space in yourself and your life for true happiness to appear.

There have been many times in my own life when I haven't been completely honest with myself and/or the world, and I'll be spilling the excruciating details throughout this book. Every time I've faked it, it's been because I thought it would make me feel better but, instead, every time I've lived to regret it, just like Rachel. If the same is true for you, don't feel bad. It's completely understandable to want to protect yourself from hurt, it's just that pretending to be something or someone you're not isn't the answer. In order to live a happy, authentic life, you need to rediscover who you truly are. So let's make a start right now, by finding out who you *were* . . .

The truth sets me free #TrueFace

2
WHO WERE YOU?

----------- ★ -----------

One of the lessons that I grew up with was
to always stay true to yourself and never let
what somebody else says distract you from
your goals.

Michelle Obama

When I was a child, we didn't have a TV – and this was in the days before internet and mobile phones! But don't worry, this book hasn't suddenly morphed into a misery memoir: one thing we did have plenty of was books. Millions of them. Or at least to my small self it certainly felt that way. Every available inch of wall or floor space in our house was covered with books. Even the landing half way up the stairs was home to two teetering sets of shelves. So I had a choice – either I died of boredom or I read.

So I read – and read and read – and pretty soon words became my passion. I loved the way they could build whole worlds to escape into and create characters who felt like old friends. The highlight of my week was on Saturday morning, when my mum would take my siblings and me to the local library and I got to choose a grand total of *six* new books to devour. When I wasn't reading, I was writing little books made from folded-up paper – usually about families of talking mice who lived in the roots of oak trees or girls who went to boarding schools and spent an inordinate amount of time having midnight feasts. I also dreamt of a day when I'd write proper books with proper covers and a shelf of their own.

Then, when I went to university to study English Literature and my dream of becoming a writer seemed to be inching closer, I had a massive crisis of confidence. The other aspiring writers on my course were all from much wealthier backgrounds than me. I was the only one from a council estate; the only one, it seemed, whose parents didn't have some kind of connections in the publishing world. And so I buried my passion for writing, dropped out of uni and went to work in a shop. Now the fact that you're reading this book and it has a proper cover and isn't made out of folded-up paper and doesn't feature any talking mice shows that I did eventually manage to overcome my fear and reignite my love of words. But for several years, I lived in a weird kind of personal wilderness where I pretended that my main passion in life was to party and I barely read or wrote a word.

Awaken your Sleeping Beauty

Do you remember the fairy tale, 'Sleeping Beauty'? In a nutshell, a wicked fairy places a curse on a beautiful princess, causing her to sleep for one hundred years when she pricks her finger on a spindle. As the princess sleeps, a thick forest of trees and brambles springs up around the castle, preventing anyone from entering. This fairy tale forms the perfect analogy for what happens when we deny our true selves in some way. We build a thick wall of fear around us to block out our dreams, and our true selves go to sleep for one hundred years. Or at least it can feel that long.

But all is not lost.

The ending of 'Sleeping Beauty' is actually a great lesson in how to overcome fear and rediscover our true self. When the Prince (a metaphor for our own courage, not a romantic partner) prepares to brave the forest (our fears), the trees and brambles part before him. He finds the Princess (our true self) and with a kiss (love) he reawakens her – and she lives happily ever after. To simplify it:

courage + self-love = true self reawakened

When my friend Sarah was little she loved nothing more than raiding the dressing-up box and putting on plays. Often, I'd be cast in her plays – usually as the victim of a terrible murder or tragic drugs overdose (the TV soap *EastEnders* was Sarah's favourite muse). It was clear to everyone who knew her that Sarah was a born performer; the D in her DNA most definitely stood for Drama.

Fast-forward a few years, and Sarah is now working as an occupational therapist. She is a very good occupational therapist but she is the first to admit that she could never describe her job as her passion. When I pushed her to tell me what her passion was, she replied, 'Well, I suppose it would still be acting.' But when I suggested that Sarah join a local amateur dramatics society as a way of re-connecting with that passion, she instantly hit me with a fear avalanche:

'What if I'm no good? I don't think I could take the stress of having to learn lines.'

'What if I am good and I get given a lead role? I'd never cope with the pressure.'

It was like watching a forest of trees and brambles spring up all around her, as the drama-loving Sarah disappeared before my eyes.

Find a True Face photo

What dreams and passions have you buried? Which part of you pricked her finger on fear and fell fast asleep? In order to awaken the Sleeping Beauty within, you'll need to do a bit of digging to rediscover who she was – and still is.

A really powerful starting point for this process is to have a dig through some early childhood photos. A couple of years after I dropped out of uni, I came across a picture of myself aged about three. In it, I am wearing a cosy-looking duffel coat and clutching a rag doll. Pale winter sunshine is causing my hair to glow gold and my skin is as clear as porcelain. I am smiling shyly at the camera. I look happy and innocent and beautiful.

This might not sound like much of a big deal to you but studying this photo had a profound effect on me. There was so much pain and stress in my childhood, I had let it come to define me. By the time I'd got to my twenties, I didn't look back on myself as a happy, innocent or beautiful child at all. I looked back on my childhood as something I had to survive, not thrive in. My parents' marriage was a battleground. Their divorce was apocalyptic. By the time I was fifteen I was drinking and taking drugs to numb the pain. I'd redefined myself as unlovable and unattractive. I was deeply unhappy.

And yet here was this picture of me as a sweet, smiling child, glowing with happiness and innocence. As I looked into my younger self's hopeful gaze, I felt myself spiralling back in time and I found myself remembering far more positive things.

At the age of three, I'd had such a sense of wonder at the world and a *huge* imagination. This was massively inspired by my mum. She would take me out to play in the woods and tell me that fairies lived in the old tree stumps. When we came across a ring of toadstools she told me that's where the fairies went to dance. When we went to the park, my mum wouldn't just stand there, watching me play or chatting to the other mums, she always helped me create imaginary worlds to explore. I would wriggle under the climbing frame and pretend to be a monkey in a cage and my mum would feed me jelly babies through the bars.* The park swings would become soaring eagles or spaceships for me to ride on. The roundabout would spin me off into different magical worlds. I was

---

* In case you were wondering, 'scientific studies' have shown that jelly babies are a monkey's favourite food.

constantly creating stories in my head inspired by my surroundings, and I was constantly being encouraged to do so.

As my closed-off, twenty-something self continued gazing at the photo I was struck by another thought – was this my true self I was looking at? This free-spirited, imaginative child.

At the time the picture was taken, nothing very bad had happened to me. My parents were still in love and my spirit/personality/character/soul, call it what you like, was still as unblemished as my snowy-white skin. Tears started rolling down my face as I realised how disconnected I'd become from the real me. I put the picture in a frame and placed it next to my bed. I wanted a daily visual reminder because I wanted to get back to that fun-loving, imaginative person. This was to become my vital first step in rediscovering my True Face.

See if you can find a similar picture of yourself taken at a young age – a picture that captures your innocence, hope and joy – a picture that captures your True Face. Let it remind you of how you would greet a day, choose to play, and view the world. Let it remind you of *you*. Put it somewhere you'll see it regularly so that it becomes a North Star, guiding you on your journey back to that person.

Now let's start delving a little deeper.

The *When I Was Little* List

- -

At the top of a fresh page in your journal, write:

When I was little I loved . . .

And start listing all the things you used to love to do.

Here's mine to help prompt you:

When I was little I loved . . .

★ Reading. Reading. Reading.

★ Writing stories in little books made from folded-up paper.

★ Riding my bike.

★ Making up adventures with my imaginary friends (called Datchoo and Gantry!).

★ Listening to music and making up my own tunes on the flute.

★ Making cakes so I could lick the bowl.

★ Playing with my doll's house – and the toy monkey who lived on the roof.

★ Racing toy cars and taking them to be repaired in my toy garage.

★ Anne of Green Gables and Pippi Longstocking.

★ Playing hide and seek in the woods – playing *anything* in the woods.

★ Going on summer holidays to Ireland.

★ Blackberry picking.

★ Building sandcastles decorated with seaweed and shells.

★ Chasing waves on the beach.

★ Pretending I was a detective like Nancy Drew and recording clues in my notebook.

★ Playing at being a dance teacher and bribing my younger siblings with sweets to be my students.

★ Dressing up in weird and wonderful outfits – and

going out in public in them.

★ Pretending to be a taxi driver!

Now it's your turn. When you were little what did you love to do? Where did you love to play? What did you love to play with? What games did you invent? Did you have any imaginary friends? Who were they? Who did you pretend to be? What did you love to create? What did you love to wear? Where was your favourite escape? What was your favourite book? Who was your favourite hero or heroine? What did you love to eat? What are your happiest memories?

You should definitely be grinning by the end of your list. Being a kid is fun – and it's fun because we let our imaginations rule and we aren't bothered about what other people think of us. If we want to be a pirate we make a cutlass out of cardboard and yell, 'hoy there, me hearties!' If we want to be a taxi driver we tape a transistor radio to the handlebars of our bike and cycle our teddy bear to the imaginary airport at the end of the road. One of the greatest tragedies of becoming an adult is that we allow our imaginations to become stifled and we allow fear to put our dreams to sleep. Enjoy delving back through the forest and rediscovering your true self.

Play time

- -

Once you've completed your list, pick one thing from it to re-create now. If you'd written that you used to love pretending to be a rock star, then dig out your air guitar and start rocking. If you'd written that you used to love playing hide and seek then enlist the help of some younger friends or relatives and start counting to twenty. Don't worry about not looking cool – we live in a world where having the body of a starvation victim is considered cool. 'Cool' as dictated by the media is subjective, dubious and often dangerous. From now on, you'll be making your own cool – and you'll soon learn that if you do anything with enough sass and flair, it won't be long before others will want to join in.

When I did this exercise, I chose riding a bike. Now, this might seem a bit lame if you cycle regularly, but at that point I hadn't ridden a bike for over ten years. Part of me was terrified that I wouldn't know how to do it any more and would go flying head over handlebars. So I borrowed a friend's bike and took it deep into some woods near where I lived – so no one would see me if I did fall off. But, after a bit of a wobbly start – and nearly flattening a poor squirrel – I was soon tearing through the trees with the wind in my hair. And it was brilliant. I felt exactly that same sense of freedom I'd felt when I was seven, taking my teddy bear to the pretend airport in my pretend taxi. I came home feeling energised and ready to take on anything.

Searching for clues

Hopefully by now you've built up a clear picture of everything that made you happy as a young child. Now, for the final exercise in this section, I want you to study your groundwork, your *When I was little I loved* . . . list, and do a little digging for clues.

Start circling all the things that still make you smile today. For example, it could be that when you were little you loved making models out of Play-Doh.

You may very well have grown out of your Play-Doh phase by now but if the thought of being creative still appeals to you, circle it. If not, move on to the next thing on your list. Once you have gone through them all, I want you to make a final, definitive list of the things you've circled, titled: **My True Passions**. We'll be coming back to this list later so keep it somewhere safe.

Now we're starting to rediscover who you truly are, we need to take a look at what might be preventing you from presenting your True Face to the world. It's time to find out what masks you might be wearing, what caused them, and how these painful experiences can actually be to your advantage . . .

I am courageous enough to rediscover my true self
#TrueFace

3
TAKING OFF YOUR MASK

------------ ★ ------------

Turn your wounds into wisdom.

Oprah Winfrey

As you now know, when I was little, I was a book-reading, sweet-eating, flute-playing, story-creating, dancing, bike-riding, wannabe taxi driver. Then, when I was fifteen years old, something happened that made me cover up my true self and my true feelings in a big way. My mum and dad split up and my mum moved out. This was how I truly felt back then:

★ Heartbroken – *I wanted to cry all the time.*

★ Frightened – *I desperately needed someone to give me a hug and tell me it was all going to be okay.*

★ Alone – *there was nobody I could talk to about how I was feeling.*

★ Sad – *I felt like I had lost the person I was closest to.*

But, rather than show my True Face to the world, I chose to cover it up. The night before my mum left, I lay in bed, unable to sleep. Part of me wanted to run through to her room and tell her I loved her and beg her to stay. But another part of me felt certain that it was too late – she'd made her decision and she wasn't going to change her mind. If I begged her to stay and she refused it would only make my pain a million times worse. So I continued to lie there, crying quietly in the dark. The next day, when my mum left, my younger siblings were openly heartbroken but according to my dad, I just sat in the living room, staring into space. I had put my mask on – and I wouldn't be taking it off again for a very long time. This is the mask I chose to wear:

★ Rebel – *I started skipping school and hanging round with a group of older friends.*

★ Tough – *I dyed my hair purple and got my ears pierced multiple times.*

★ Party-mad – *I started drinking and smoking and going to clubs.*

★ Experienced – *I told friends at school I'd lost my virginity (when I hadn't!).*

Basically, I invented a rebellious, street-smart persona for my frightened, hurt self to hide behind. Skipping school and hanging round with older people and going to clubs when I was underage might sound cool and exciting but the reality was, I often felt frightened and out of my depth.

For example, one night just before Christmas, when I was fifteen, my friend and I had decided to go to a club in London's West End. Earlier that day, we'd spent hours in Top Shop on Oxford Circus choosing the perfect dresses for the occasion. Hers was bright red and made her look like Madonna in the 'Material Girl' video; and mine was black velvet and tight and made me feel like a film star. Our dresses bought us entry into one of the top clubs in London. It should have been a great night.

It wasn't.

We drank and danced our butts off for hours and by the end of the night, everything was a hazy blur of disco lights and dry ice. Then a man grabbed hold of me for what I thought was a dance. The next thing I knew, I felt a searing pain in my neck. For some bizarre reason, the random man had launched himself upon me and given me a 'love bite'. It was so painful and shocking that I ended up in tears. I was fifteen. *Fifteen.* Over the next few days, a violent bruise erupted on my neck, turning my skin angry shades of red, purple and blue.

Now, I know some people wear love bites like

badges of honour but there had been nothing 'loving' about this bite and I felt as if I'd been branded – branded as cheap and easy. Instead of placing the responsibility with the man, or with the other adults who had allowed me to get into this position in the first place, I blamed myself. A fifteen-year-old girl. Every time I looked at the bruise on my neck I saw myself as pathetic for getting into such a horrible situation, but I didn't know how to explain or articulate it, so I pretended I didn't care and my true self retreated further behind my mask.

Seeing beneath the mask

A while ago, I was running a workshop on the theme of Dare to Dream. One of the participants – a young woman in her early twenties – made an instant impression when she entered the room talking (loudly) on her phone. 'He's seeing three people at the moment – and one of them is his best friend's girlfriend!' was the line that grabbed everyone's attention.

Once she had finished dissecting her friend's tangled

love life, she proceeded to talk (equally loudly) to the person sitting next to her about the fact that she'd just been for a smear test. With the killer line 'apparently, I've got an elusive cervix', once again, she captured the attention of the entire room.

Throughout the first few exercises, this woman spoke the loudest, laughed the most and frequently interrupted the other participants. She had a clear and obvious desire to be centre stage. Then, something very interesting happened. I did an exercise with the group in which I got them to write about their deepest fears and I asked if any of them would like to share what they had written. For once, the woman remained quiet. One by one, the participants shared their stories with searing honesty, until she was the only one who hadn't spoken. I gently asked her if she would like to share what she had written. The woman looked really uncertain, in fact her entire body language had changed. The larger-than-life character she'd arrived as had shrunk down to a much more natural size.

Slowly, and hesitantly, she began to read. Her voice was softer this time, and there was no brash laughter. The whole group listened, rapt, as she shared how her father had died from cancer when she was just five years old. A couple of years after his death, her mother had remarried – to a father of three young children. This new blended family should have been a 'happily ever after' for the girl and her mum, but the reality was far from the truth. Her new step-dad made it very clear from the outset that he favoured his own daughters over her. Not only had she suffered the loss of her dad, but every day that loss was compounded by the fact that she felt she'd become invisible and unheard.

'My greatest fear is not being listened to,' she finished, in a small voice. Instantly, the group rallied round with warmth and support. For the first time since the workshop began, we were getting to see the woman's True Face and people responded to her honesty and courage with positivity and love. The woman's childhood fear of not being noticed had led to her creating a crazy-loud mask to wear, but this wasn't who she really was at all. For the rest of the workshop, she remained much quieter and she seemed much happier. At the end, she hung back to thank me. 'I haven't felt this calm in ages,' she added, looking genuinely surprised.

Masks never fit

- -

One of the saddest and most ironic things about putting on masks to cover our hurt is that they only ever end up adding to our pain. Like wearing a skirt that is too tight, we end up feeling self-conscious and uncomfortable. Maintaining a larger-than-life persona when it's not your true self, like the woman at the workshop, becomes totally exhausting. Examining the painful incidents in our lives and how they've made us create our masks can be really uncomfortable at the time but it is essential if we want to get back to who we truly are. Think of it as a temporary pain for a long-term gain.

When I created my tough, street-smart mask to hide behind, it didn't just make me feel out of my depth when it came to men. I didn't feel as if I truly fitted in with my older friends, either. They were all in college or working. I was constantly trying to avoid doing or saying anything that would make me look like an immature school kid. And hanging round with older people made me feel lonely and out of place when I went into school because I felt as if I had nothing in common with my classmates any more. Basically, beneath the piercings and the swagger and the permanent halo of cigarette smoke, I was a total stress-head!

It's important to point out here that creating a mask to hide behind is not something to feel bad about. It's a natural defence mechanism that we've all used at some point or another, so please don't beat yourself up over it. I truly believed that becoming tough and street-wise would stop me from ever getting hurt again. My mum leaving had been such a massive shock – I really hadn't seen it coming and I never wanted to be that vulnerable or unprepared for pain again. I thought I needed to put on an act in order to protect myself.

I can totally see why I did it but I now know that I was wrong. In order to live your happiest, most authentic life, you need to become your happiest, most authentic self. And that means ditching the masks. And actually, ditching the masks can make you a whole lot stronger and can even be to your advantage. Before you fling this book down, yelling, 'There's nothing advantageous about getting dumped/ my parents' divorce/my so-called best friend doing the dirty on me!' please take a moment to hear me out.

Filling the cracks with gold

Did you know that in Japan, they have a tradition for mending broken ornaments by filling the cracks with gold? No dull old superglue for them! This is because the Japanese believe that when something's been damaged and has a history it makes it all the more beautiful, and they want to emphasise that beauty. This can be quite a hard concept to get your head around at first, so I'm going to say it again:

When some- thing's been damaged and has a history it makes it all the more beautiful.

If you've just suffered the pain of your parents' divorce or been left devastated by a break-up it's probably very difficult to see how this has made you more beautiful – especially if your eyes are still as puffy and pink as marshmallows from days of crying. But the truth is, it *has* left you more beautiful – or at least, it's left you with the potential to be more beautiful. Experiencing pain can make us more compassionate, understanding and loving. It can strengthen us, make us better able to cope with future challenges, and give us a healthier perspective on life – if we allow it. And this is the crucial point:

We might not have any choice over what life throws at us, but we always have the choice over how we react.

Oprah Winfrey is a great example of this. She was born into poverty in rural Mississippi, to a single, teenage mum. She was raped at the age of nine. By the time she was fourteen she'd given birth to a son, who died in infancy. Oprah could have let these traumatic experiences crush her, or she could have created a hardened mask to hide behind. Instead she followed her passion of becoming a broadcaster and landed a job in radio while she was still at high school. By the time she was nineteen she was co-hosting the local evening news. The emotional, honest way in which she spoke to the listeners won her a job in TV, taking a little-known chat show in Chicago to record viewing figures. Oprah went on to become an actress, producer and mega-successful businesswoman who now owns her own television network. She has also dedicated her life, career and millions of dollars to helping others improve their lives. She has turned the damage caused by her childhood into gold.

'I had no idea that being my authentic self could make me as rich as I've become,' Oprah says. 'If I had, I'd have done it a lot earlier.'

Digging for gold

Now it's time to identify anything that's happened in your life that's made you pretend to be something or someone you're not. It doesn't have to be as dramatic as a parent moving out – it could be a putdown by a teacher that you haven't managed to shake off. Or it could be something that happened with your friends that made you feel awkward, embarrassed or bad about yourself. Basically, we're looking for anything that made you stop being your true self by holding back or changing in some way. To help you uncover these moments, complete these quick-fire writing prompts in your journal:

A really embarrassing memory I still cringe about is ...

A really painful experience was ...

I was really hurt when ...

I get really angry when I remember ...

I still cry when I think of ...

Once you have a list of incidents that have caused you discomfort or pain, free-write (that means write down whatever comes into your mind – don't feel you have to use proper sentences or phrases, or even stick to the lines on the page! You can even draw your feelings if that's easier and feels more comfortable for you) in your journal beneath each of the following subheadings for each one:

My painful incident

How it made me feel

What it made me do

How it made me change

When you've reflected on that, hopefully you can identify:

My true feelings and my mask

Now, I want you to go back to each of your painful incidents and answer the following question:

How has my mask hurt me rather than helped?

The reason for this question is simple – you put on your mask because you thought it would make you feel better, so you're not going to take it off until you can see how it's actually been making you feel worse.

Turning your wounds into wisdom

Looking at your list of painful incidents and the ways in which they have caused you to put on masks, and the ways in which these masks have hurt, have a think about how you can turn your own pain to gold. How can these experiences make you a better, stronger, more caring person? How can you follow Oprah's example and 'turn your wounds into wisdom'? How could they help you to help others? At the top of a fresh page in your journal write:

How can I turn my wounds into wisdom?

and free-write whatever comes into your mind.

In my own case, although my mum leaving caused a deep emotional wound, it has also helped me in many ways. Having to look after myself from the age of fifteen gave me an inner strength and sense of independence that has seen me well through the various challenges of adulthood.

But most importantly, it taught me about the importance of forgiveness. I was very angry at my mum for leaving for many years but eventually I learnt that this was only prolonging our pain and keeping us apart. This was a great life lesson and a real source of wisdom.

Warrior wisdom

Now it's time to turn all the things you've learnt into a short, snappy bolt of wisdom. I call these words your 'warrior wisdom' because they come straight from your emotional battle scars.

Go through your answer to the previous question and underline or highlight the key words and phrases that sum up how your pain has made you learn and/ or grow. Then condense these words into one or two sentences, beginning with: '*I have learnt . . .*' Using my personal experience as an illustration, I would write something like: '*I have learnt that I am incredibly strong and self-sufficient; and that forgiveness sets you free.*'

Once you've completed this exercise, reward yourself with a massive hug (it is actually possible to hug yourself and I thoroughly recommend it!). You've done a lot of hard work in this chapter, and gone over some painful ground. But you've learnt how to turn your pain into gold and your wounds into wisdom and this new understanding will fill you with strength, sensitivity and beauty – after all, there's nothing more beautiful than someone with an open and compassionate heart.

Although what happened to me as a teenager really hurt at the time – and the mask I put on ended up causing me even more pain – I've ultimately emerged from it a lot stronger and wiser. I use what I've learnt from the experience pretty much every day in my work as a life coach and writer – helping other people trust in their truth and remove their masks. Putting your pain to work to help others is one of the most fulfilling things you can do – as you will also discover.

I will fill my emotional cracks with gold **#TrueFace**

4

DISCOVERING YOUR STAR QUALITIES

----------- ★ -----------

'Born This Way' is about being yourself and loving who you are and being proud.

Lady Gaga

So, how are you feeling right now? If you had to give your happiness a score out of ten (with zero being *rainy-Monday-morning-grim* and ten being *soaring-first-day-of-holiday-joy*) what would it be? It could be that the last chapter has left you feeling a little five or six-ish. If so, fear not. You have just arrived at Chapter Feel Good. This chapter's mission is to remind you of what a unique, fantastic and out-and-out wonderful person you are. Welcome, dear *True Facer*, to Your Star Qualities.

Did you know that you are made of stardust? And no, this is not some ridiculously cheesy metaphor, it's actually true.

I interrupt this book to bring you a hardcore scientific fact. During a supernova (the massive explosion that occurs at the end of a star's life) stardust is sent scattering across the universe, going on to form the building blocks of planets and everything on them. Like Earth. And us.

When I first found out this fact, it caused a mini supernova in my mind. There was I thinking that I was just made of plain old flesh and blood when actually I am – and you are – made of stardust. So, when I talk about your Star Qualities, I'm not talking

'Hollywood star' or 'celebrity star', I'm talking about the qualities you possess deep inside that will enable you to shine. Do you remember the equations back in Chapter One?

Self-doubt + pressure to be accepted = temptation to fake

self-belief + self-acceptance = True Face

In order to live a happy and authentic life you have to learn to love and accept yourself for who you *are*, not who you think you *ought to be*. One of the best ways you can turn self-doubt into self-belief is by shifting your focus away from your fears and on to your Star Qualities.

Let me give you an example. A few years ago, I was running a workshop for writers, helping them get focused on their writing resolutions. Once I had got the writers present to jot down a list of all their writing goals, I asked them to write another list – this time of all the fears they experienced when it came to these goals. They all started writing away furiously. Some of them had entire pages of fears. Then I asked them to write a list of all the things they were proud of achieving in their lives. This could be anything,

I told them, not just writing-related. But despite this, they seemed to find it a lot harder to write this list.

'Does it have to be things we're proud of?' one woman asked. 'Could it be things we're *quite pleased* with achieving?' Her question made me sad because it highlighted how we've been conditioned to have an aversion to pride. 'Pride comes before a fall,' so the saying goes. But I believe that pride in its truest meaning, actually *prevents* a fall. We're conditioned not to feel proud for fear of appearing arrogant or boastful but being proud doesn't mean showing off. According to the Oxford English Dictionary, being proud means '*a feeling of deep pleasure or satisfaction as a result of one's own achievements or qualities*'. Taking a quiet, private moment to reflect upon all you've achieved can really help counteract the people and situations that knock your self-esteem.

But to get the writers to complete the exercise I told them that yes, they could write a list of things they were 'quite pleased' with achieving. They all started writing – and they all finished writing a whole lot quicker than they did with their list of fears. Then I went around the group getting them to read their writing goals, followed by their 'pleased with achieving' list, followed by their fears.

The first person who spoke was a young woman

called Sangeeta. Her writing goal was to complete her first novel. One of the things she was most pleased with achieving was coming to the UK from India at the age of eighteen, not speaking a word of English, and yet making friends and feeling totally at home within a couple of years. Her biggest fear when it came to her writing was the fear of having her novel rejected. This fear was so paralysing that she actually couldn't even comprehend sending the manuscript out to agents, and this in turn was making her reluctant to write – what was the point if she was never going to do anything with it?

When I heard Sangeeta's story I gave a little whoop inside because I knew that it would form the perfect example for the rest of the group and that's why I'm sharing it with you here. I got Sangeeta to tell us a bit more about what it was like coming to a strange country at the age of eighteen. She spoke vividly and movingly about how isolating and frightening it was not being able to understand a word of what was being said around her and how lonely she had felt in those first few months.

'So how did things begin to improve?' I asked. Sangeeta explained how she had worked really hard at learning to speak English and how she had taken every possible opportunity to get to know new people and make friends, even when she felt nervous and shy.

'And what qualities did you need to achieve that, to create a whole new life for yourself?' I asked. She thought about it for a moment. It was clearly the first time she had considered it in this way.

'Determination?' she replied, questioningly.

I nodded.

'Courage?'

Yep.

'Self-belief?'

By this time the whole group was nodding and yes-ing along.

'So, you're brave enough and determined enough to travel half way round the world to create a new life for yourself *at the age of eighteen*,' I said, 'but when it comes to sending out a manuscript . . . ?'

We all looked at Sangeeta. Sangeeta started to laugh. 'Okay.'

'Okay, what?'

'Okay, I can do it.'

And she did do it. She now has three books published in the UK and India with a fourth on the way. But if she hadn't stopped to remind herself that one of her Star Qualities is courage (in spades) then she might never have sent that first manuscript out.

Finding your own Star Qualities

Having uncovered your true passions, explored your painful experiences and identified the masks you might be wearing, it's now time to move a little deeper into the heart of who you are. This next exercise will help you unearth your own personal Star Qualities. It's really important that you do this exercise when you know you're not going to be interrupted so that you can take the time to respond as fully as possible. It will probably take up to an hour to complete. Turn to a fresh page in your journal and write the question:

What ten things am I most proud of achieving?

As I said before, being proud doesn't mean showing off – it's just a quiet, inner recognition of the things you've done well. And you're not writing this list to be published on the internet or broadcast over the tannoy in your local shopping centre, it's for you and you alone, so please write as freely as you can. It might help to write the following subheadings in your journal:

Academic/Work

These can be any achievements that you're proud of relating to school or work, i.e. exam results, particular pieces of work that you're proud of completing, jobs that you've done well in, being elected to the school council or being part of a sports team. Or it could be that you've intervened when someone was getting bullied or that you've been a mentor for a younger student.

Family

It could be that you're proud of being a really great sibling – the kind who shares her clothes and make-up with her sister and never shouts at her little brother (not even when he gave your favourite doll an unauthorised haircut!). Or maybe you're proud of how well you get on with your parents – or how you've dealt with any issues to do with your parents, such as their divorce.

Friends

When it comes to feeling proud regarding your friends, it could be that you're an awesome, caring friend, or it could be that you've handled certain issues that have come up in your friendships really well. Maybe you've mediated between two friends when they had a falling-out? Maybe you always provide a shoulder for your friends to cry on? Or maybe you've had to deal with being left out or picked on by certain friends and feel proud of how you coped?

Personal

Personal achievements can be anything from how you've acted in a romantic/relationship scenario to overcoming issues such as shyness or self-doubt.

And to help you dig deeper, try these other questions as prompts:

What have you been thanked for?

When have you put somebody's needs before your own?

How have you made somebody laugh?

What's the best present you ever gave someone?

When have you had to be really brave?

What are two of the best things you've created?

What do your friends like most about you?

What's the nicest thing anyone's ever said to you?

List three occasions when you've helped someone.

Star Qualities

- -

Once you have your list of ten things that you're proud of – and if you've thought of more than ten, even better – jot down the qualities you needed to achieve each one. For example, if you wrote that you're proud of learning to swim despite a fear of water, the qualities you needed could have been courage and determination. Or, if you're proud of the way you helped a friend get over a painful incident in her life, the qualities you needed could have been compassion, understanding and love. If the best present you ever gave someone was a poem you wrote about how much you loved them, then write down the qualities love, kindness and creativity.

Complete this exercise for each of your achievements, making sure that you list as many qualities as you can think of for each one. Then compile them in a separate list titled Star Qualities. It is so important that you acknowledge your qualities in this way. By writing them in a list like this, you're underlining to yourself that you do possess them. And this in turn should make you feel a whole lot better about yourself.

True Face Manifesto

- -

Before we move on, we need to take stock. So far, you've been working like a detective, gathering clues about yourself. Now it's time to put all of the evidence together so that you can become super-clear on exactly who you are.

Gather together your TRUE PASSIONS, PAINFUL INCIDENTS, WARRIOR WISDOM and STAR QUALITIES. Then turn to a fresh page in your journal and write at the top:

MY TRUE FACE MANIFESTO

Beneath it, write the following sentence openings, followed by each of your findings:

My name is:

And I love to: (*enter your* **True Passions** *here*)

I am: (*enter your* **Star Qualities** *here*)

I have experienced: (*enter your* **Painful Incidents** *here*)

And it has made me stronger, wiser and more beautiful because: (*enter your* **Warrior Wisdom** *here*)

If there's room, attach your True Face photo to the page. We will be coming back to this manifesto throughout the second part of this book, as we work together on creating your truly authentic life. It will provide a great source of inspiration whenever you set out to achieve a goal and it will also be a powerful antidote to anyone or anything that stands in your way. Speaking of which, before we move on, we need to face up to what could be the biggest obstacle you'll encounter on your quest to living a True Face life. This fiend is the dastardly villain to your heroine; the Voldemort to your Hermione. And no, I'm not talking about the teacher or boss who always has it in for you, or the parent who's always nagging. I'm not even talking about the school bully or two-faced friend from hell. I'm talking about something way closer to home – your Inner Voice of Doom.

My body is made of stardust and I am made to shine **#TrueFace**

5

SILENCING YOUR INNER VOICE OF DOOM

----------- ★ -----------

We have to reshape our own perception of how we see ourselves.

Beyoncé

You've just got ready to go out and you're checking yourself in the mirror. You're wearing a new top that looked great when you tried it on in the shop, but suddenly you hear a voice in your head saying: *You can't go out in that! It makes you look so fat!*

You're daydreaming about your perfect career. It's making you feel excited and alive and inspired, when suddenly that same voice says: *Oh my God! You would never be able to do that. You're not nearly good enough.*

You've met a boy you really like. He's funny, cute and smart and he seems to like you too. You're busy dreaming up a soft-focus, rom-com style montage of you both, skipping hand-in-hand through autumn leaves, meandering through a museum and dining by candlelight when that voice pipes up again: *Ha! There's no way he'd like you. You're way too ugly. You're not interesting enough. And you have a spot on your chin. People with spots on their chin never get dates!*

Let me to introduce you to your Inner Voice of Doom. Of course, you've been hearing this voice for a very long time. It will have started its morbid commentary pretty much as soon as you were old enough to realise that society expects you to look and be perfect in every way, *all the frickin' time.* But the chances are, you don't really know your Inner Voice of Doom, and by that I mean, you don't know what lies behind it and why it says the things that it does.

I didn't for a long, long time. I just accepted that it was part of my life; an ever-present, doom-laden commentator who seemed intent on spoiling all my fun. And never does our Inner Voice of Doom get louder or more doom-laden than when we are first trying to live in a True Face way.

As I wrote earlier, all through my childhood, I dreamt of one day becoming a writer. Then, when I was seventeen I realised that if I was serious about this dream I ought to start working at getting a place at university. So I stopped skiving off school and started hanging out in the library instead of pubs and clubs. For a whole year, I stayed focused on my goal and it paid off. When I passed my A levels I was so happy. Now I had a place at uni to study English Literature, hopefully my dream of becoming a writer would one day come true.

But about a year into my degree, my Inner Voice of Doom started having a field day. As I mentioned before, most of the other aspiring writers on my course already seemed to have contacts in the publishing or journalism worlds. In contrast, I had no contacts – on the council estate I came from girls didn't become writers or journalists when they left school. And so, my Inner Voice of Doom started to taunt me with the following statements:

You can't be a writer.

You're not good enough.

You're not rich enough.

You don't know enough people in the industry.

You don't know anyone in the industry.

You're from a council estate.

People from council estates don't become writers.

You should just leave uni and go and work in a shop.

So that's what I did. I left uni after two years and went to work in a shop. And when the shop went out of business, I ended up going to work for the complaints department at a frozen food company, where the only thing I wrote were grovelling apology letters about cockroaches found in ice-cream.

What I wish I'd known back then is that we don't have to let our Inner Voice of Doom run the show – there are actually really effective ways of getting it to be quiet. It took me seven years to figure this out though. Seven years of working in crappy office jobs that made me want to staple myself to death from boredom. So, this chapter is *very* important. It could end up saving you from years of frustration, not to mention Death by Stapler.

From childhood dreams to teenage doubts

When we are very little, self-doubt is pretty much non-existent. Picture the scene: four-year-olds Johnny and Rosie are playing dressing-up. Johnny asks Rosie what she wants to be. Rosie is currently fascinated by the moon and stars so she goes straight for the astronaut's costume. Then she hesitates.

'What's up?' Johnny asks as he pulls on his pirate's eye-patch.

'I don't think I can do this,' Rosie replies gravely. 'No one in my family is an astronaut. I don't know any astronauts. I'm not clever enough to be an astronaut. And anyway, that spacesuit is going to make me look *so fat*!'

This scenario just wouldn't happen. Because when we are four we are still pretty much our true selves. We still let our imagination be our guide and we haven't yet cultivated an Inner Voice of Doom. If anything, at four years old, the only inner voice we have cultivated is one of fun, which says things like, *I love the moon and stars. I'm going to be an astronaut and spend my whole life looping the loop around Mars.*

When college administrator Jenny was a young child she loved animals. Her bedroom was a menagerie of toy pets and one of her favourite games was pretending to be a vet and treating her toys for a variety of ailments.

'Whenever anyone asked me what I wanted to be when I was older, I would always reply "veterinary surgeon" in a very serious voice,' Jenny says. 'I had that unquestioning self-belief that all small children have – animals were what I loved, so it seemed only natural to me that I should become a vet.'

This unquestioning self-belief that Jenny talks about is one of the best aspects of being a young child.

But when Jenny reached thirteen, her Inner Voice of Doom started taking over big time.

'When I went to high school I started being bullied,' she explains, 'and it really shook my confidence. The worst thing was, it wasn't just the bullies who were saying mean things to and about me – my own inner voice started joining in too. Whenever I thought about becoming a vet, my inner voice would say things like, *You're not good enough at science to be a vet and anyway, who would want to employ you?* Instead of having an unquestioning belief that I could achieve my dream, I started listening to my Inner Voice of Doom and developed an unquestioning belief that I couldn't.'

This is the real tragedy of giving your Inner Voice of Doom too much power – it can block you from living the life you should be living and force you into becoming a timid, smaller version of your true self. Although Jenny now goes horse-riding every weekend and has a pet dog, she still has wistful moments, wondering how different her life might have been if she'd pursued her dream of working with animals.

Who is your Inner Voice of Doom?

The saddest thing about your Inner Voice of Doom is that it actually belongs to you. It's you saying all those mean things – to *you*! Take a moment to think of something your Inner Voice of Doom likes to say to you, then imagine saying that same thing to your best friend or a loved one. The first time I did this exercise I was horrified. If a friend or loved one of mine told me that they wanted to become a writer, there is no way I would start saying, *Oh my God, you can't do that! You're not clever enough! You're not good enough!* And I'm sure you're exactly the same. So why do we say these things to ourselves? Why is our Inner Voice of Doom so mean?

Answer: Because it is afraid.

That's right. Our evil, bullying Inner Voice of Doom is actually terrified and, believe it or not, it really wants to protect us. It just has a very odd way of going about it!

When I got to uni and realised that my fellow students were from very different backgrounds from my own, part of me became really scared. When I imagined myself competing against these people for jobs in the publishing or media worlds, I became convinced that I would fail. I'm ashamed to say it now, but I felt that the fact that I came from a council estate meant that in some way I wasn't good enough. So, when my inner voice started doom-mongering, and telling me that I wasn't clever enough, or rich enough, it was actually trying to protect me from getting hurt. It didn't want me to apply for jobs in publishing or the media because it was scared that I would fail and have to suffer the pain of rejection.

Our Inner Voice of Doom isn't out to get us, it's out to protect us – in the most limiting way. It's what happens when we become blinded by fear. But it doesn't have to be this way. Once we become aware of what's going on and why we speak to ourselves in this way, we've won half the battle. Then we just need to change what our inner voice says.

Create an Inner Cheerleader

- -

A great way of doing this is to replace your Inner Voice of Doom with a different voice, a voice that praises and encourages you, and focuses on your achievements rather than shortcomings. It's time to welcome your Inner Cheerleader.

Now, the chances are, your Inner Cheerleader might have been very quiet in recent years. Maybe you haven't even heard from her at all. But that's fine – together we can coax her out of her shell – after all, just like your Voice of Doom, she is a part of you. And once you get her going, she'll transform your life by filling you with self-belief. Don't believe me? Then allow me to introduce you to my star witness – Beyoncé.

Beyoncé has been a successful recording artist for most of her life and if you've ever seen her strutting the stage, voice booming and hair billowing, it's probably hard to imagine her being anything other than ultra-confident. But for many years, Beyoncé battled crippling shyness. And when this shyness threatened to derail her music career, she stopped listening to her Inner Voice of Doom and created her own Inner Cheerleader – who she named Sasha Fierce.

Beyoncé describes Sasha Fierce as 'the fun, more sensual, more aggressive, more outspoken and more glamorous side of me that comes out when I'm working and on stage'. Through listening to this far feistier inner voice she has been able to silence her shyness and fear and pursue her dream with passion.

Back when I was at uni, I really needed my own version of Sasha Fierce to start whooping and hollering and drowning out my Inner Voice of Doom. I needed her to say things like:

Of course you're good enough to be a writer.

You've read about a million books!

You know what makes a good story.

Who cares where you grew up?

Council estate life is tough but it's given you loads of interesting experiences to write about.

You didn't think you'd be able to get a place at uni but you worked hard and you did.

If you work just as hard at becoming a writer you can definitely make it.

Unfortunately, I didn't know then that it was possible to create a stronger, more positive inner voice.

I allowed my Inner Voice of Doom to rule and I really regret it. But you don't have to. You can follow Beyoncé's example and create a kick-ass Inner Cheerleader to help blast away the fears holding you back from achieving your dreams. Let's start right now . . .

Favourite taunts of doom

- -

First of all, I want you to identify your Inner Voice of Doom's favourite taunts. To help you with this, I've come up with some prompts. Simply imagine the following scenarios and write down in your journal the ways in which your inner voice likes to torment you.

When you try on a new outfit . . .

When you look in the mirror before you go out . . .

When you like a guy . . .

When you are out with your friends . . .

When you are studying for an exam . . .

When you go for a job interview . . .

When you catch sight of your reflection in a shop window . . .

When you try talking to a stranger . . .

Any other favourite taunts . . .

It makes pretty depressing reading, right? But stay with me – it does get better.

What is your Inner Voice of Doom scared of?

- -

Go through each of the taunts you wrote and jot down the fear behind it. For instance, if your Inner Voice of Doom taunts you that you're not pretty enough to get a boyfriend then I would be fairly certain that there's a fear of rejection behind it. If you catch sight of your reflection in a window and your inner voice starts shouting, 'Ugly!' your fear of being judged and criticised by others is coming through. When you're studying for an exam and your inner voice whispers, 'Stupid!', your fear of failure is coming through. And when, in a new social setting, you worry that no one will want to talk to you, that's your fear of not being good enough at conversation.

How is your Inner Voice of Doom trying to protect you?

To see how your Inner Voice of Doom is actually trying to protect you (in its own bizarre way!) go back through your list, mentally changing the words 'afraid of' to 'protecting me from'. Here's another example to help you:

When Bethany catches sight of her reflection in a shop window, her Inner Voice of Doom likes to yell, 'Oh my God, you look so fat!' This is because deep down she's afraid of being made fun of for being overweight. By telling herself that she looks fat, her inner voice is issuing her with a warning. Like a nightmarish drill sergeant, it's yelling, 'You look so fat!' in order to make her take steps to protect herself from being teased. Either by going on a diet, or hiding herself away under baggier clothes.

When Bethany thinks about dating again after her recent break-up, her Inner Voice of Doom likes to say, 'Don't do it, you'll only get dumped.' It does this because it's actually terrified that she might get hurt again. And it's protecting her from going through that pain by trying to stop her from taking any more romantic risks.

Go through your Inner Voice of Doom's taunts and see how it's actually trying to protect you in each case.

Finding the mute button

- -

Now that we've established that your Inner Voice of Doom is actually an extremely, irrationally frightened, slightly dysfunctional child who's just trying to protect you in a misguided way, hopefully you can see that you don't need to take it quite so seriously. And that's my very polite way of saying, hopefully you can see that it's time to get it to shut the hell up! So without further ado, let's look at some ways in which we can put your Inner Voice of Doom on mute.

Create a Portrait of Doom

- -

I want you to create a portrait of your Inner Voice of Doom. Now bearing in mind that your voice of doom isn't nearly as evil as it sounds, this picture should be all of the following:

Comical

Childlike

Fearful

As you can see, when I drew mine it was of a giant baby, wearing a bib saying 'I ♥ DOOM!' and holding a dummy. Creating a funny, unthreatening image of your Inner Voice of Doom really helps to dilute its power and will make it a lot harder to take seriously the next time it pipes up.

Inner Cheerleader warm-up routine

Get your Inner Cheerleader limbered up with this simple exercise. Go back to your Voice of Doom taunts and rewrite them in a far more positive and empowering way.

If your Inner Voice of Doom says: *You look so fat*, your Inner Cheerleader might say: *Your curves are healthy and make you look feminine*.

If your Inner Voice of Doom says: *You'll never pass that exam*, your Inner Cheerleader might say: *You have everything it takes to pass that exam in style*.

Once you've rewritten each one, you should be starting to see how it's possible to control your inner voice – turning it from a fearful Voice of Doom to a feisty Inner Cheerleader. As we go on to explore all of the different areas of your life in the next part of this book, we will be checking in on your inner voice at regular intervals.

Okay, take a deep breath.

And another.

And smile.

If you've completed the exercises in this part of the book you should now have a clear picture of who you truly are, how you want to be feeling, all the ways in which you've learnt and grown, all the things you should be proud of, and how to stop your Inner Voice of Doom from running the show. That's a very good reason to smile. You're now ready to start creating a life that's true to you – a life crammed full of happiness and adventure. And what better place to start than spine-tingling, heart-warming LOVE . . .

My Inner Voice is my greatest cheerleader!
#TrueFace

PART TWO

♥ ♥ ♥ ♥ ♥ ♥ ♥ ♥

True Love

6

TRUE SELF-LOVE

----------- ♥ -----------

Self-love has very little to do with how you feel about your outer self. It's about accepting all of yourself.

Tyra Banks

I love myself.

It took me *a lot* of years before I was able to say that statement and really mean it. Now I can write it in a book without feeling a trace of embarrassment or doubt. I love myself. I used to think that I wasn't worthy of love. I also used to think that people who said they loved themselves were totally up themselves. How often have you heard the term 'loves themself' used as an insult. 'His problem is that he really loves himself.' 'Oh my god, she so loves herself!' It's always said with a sneer, isn't it? But when it's said in this way, it's usually being used to describe someone who's being arrogant.

There's a massive difference between loving yourself and being boastful. In fact, most people who are arrogant and boastful do so out of a *lack* of self-love. Why would they need to make such a big song and dance about themselves if they were truly happy? When you love yourself, you don't need to tell the world how great you are. You're too busy enjoying your life.

The trouble is, sometimes it can be really, really hard to love ourselves. Fear and self-doubt and our Inner Voice of Doom can all conspire to turn us into real Debbie Downers. But if you don't love your true self you won't live your best life. You'll be weighed down by feelings of worthlessness and waste all of your energy hiding your light. This in turn, can lead to various painful outcomes – like tolerating all kinds of rubbish in the name of romantic love. If you feel you are worthless, you are very likely to attract a partner who treats you as such. What's going on inside of you always shows on the outside, no matter how hard you try to disguise it. So, in order to create truly happy love lives, we need to begin with ourselves and work outwards.

The self-loathing epidemic

- -

Recently, a teenage girl in the UK killed herself after visiting a website called Ask FM. If you aren't already aware, the idea behind Ask FM is that you log on to ask and/or be asked random questions. I know this because, as an author, I sometimes get tagged when someone is asked what book they're reading. But the trouble with Ask FM is that the questions aren't always as harmless as 'What book are you reading?'

Often, they can be things like 'Why are you so ugly?' or 'Why are you so fat?' or even the terrible 'Why don't you die of cancer?'

It turned out that the British girl who killed herself had been bombarded with hateful questions such as this on the website, which caused a lot of people to ask, why go on a site like this in the first place, if you know the kind of things that will be said? The answer to that question was shocking. Apparently, a lot of girls are visiting sites where they know they will be abused, as a form of self-harm. Like picking at a scab, they feed their feelings of worthlessness by opening themselves up to abuse from strangers.

And the really tragic thing is that these kinds of sites are thriving. Recently, my friend's daughter was talking to me about some of the girls in her class.

'Linda's really sporty, Maria loves One Direction, Saskia self-harms and Lucy has a pony.'

Excuse me? It would appear that not only is self-harming reaching epidemic proportions, but it's becoming so commonplace among teenage girls that it's an activity or personal interest akin to liking a boy band.

Another symptom of self-loathing, eating disorders, are also massively on the rise. All over the world, girls and young women are bingeing, vomiting and starving themselves, sometimes to death. Now, we can blame the media, fashion and music industries until we're blue in the face – and I often do – but no one in a position of power in these industries seems to want to do very much about it. The cold, hard fact of the matter is that cold, hard cash comes before the health and well-being of young women. In the minds of most marketing executives, fashion designers and magazine editors, skinny sells – never mind that it also kills. But there is a way that we can protect ourselves from the constant bombardment by the Perfection Police, and that is to learn to truly love ourselves.

When we love ourselves, we don't want to hurt ourselves. We don't want to slash our arms with scissors, or eat nothing but Slim Fast, or go on websites filled with hate. We don't settle for second best when it comes to friendships or relationships. We honour and respect ourselves and our dreams. When we love ourselves, that love forms a protective layer around us. Like a force-field, it deflects hurtful comments and media pressure with a friendly but firm, 'Thanks, but no thanks'. The question is, why do so many young women today find it so hard to love themselves? Why do we find ourselves in the middle of an epidemic of self-loathing?

Self-love lessons

I believe that our natural state is to be loving – both to ourselves and to others. Your True Face = True Love, so somewhere along the line, something is happening to block this love. Somewhere along the line, we are being taught that actually, we are unlovable and rather than question this lesson, we internalise it so that it becomes a part of who we are.

One of my biggest self-love lessons came when my mum moved out. Despite knowing that my parents' marriage had been very unhappy for a very long time, I couldn't help viewing what happened as evidence that she didn't really love me. And as the years passed, this became etched upon my psyche like a tattoo: *My mum left me and therefore doesn't love me*. And from it came a secondary belief: *I am unlovable*.

Choose to be lovable

It's impossible to love yourself if you believe yourself to be unlovable. And once you get into this mindset, it can be really hard to snap yourself out of it. Every minor rejection, hurtful remark and setback gets used as further evidence of your 'unlovability'. Maybe not consciously, but unconsciously you begin compiling a dossier of evidence of how unlovable you think you are.

This is what I did, as a young adult. Every time I got hurt, somewhere deep down I would say to myself, 'What did you expect? You don't deserve any better.' It was very hard for me not to see these events as a lesson in my own unlovability. And the tragedy is, this way of thinking culminated in my ending up in a deeply unhappy relationship in my early twenties. Because part of me believed that I didn't deserve any better, I tolerated being cheated on and emotionally abused for a lot longer than I should have. My belief that I didn't deserve love became a self-fulfilling prophecy.

However – and thankfully this is a big however – IT DOESN'T HAVE TO BE LIKE THIS. We might not be able to control what people say about us or do to us but we always have full control over how we react.

We don't have to accept our negative self-love lessons, we can question them and see how they are false.

False love lessons

My mum does love me and she always has. Instead of choosing to interpret her moving out as evidence of how unlovable I was, I could have chosen to see it as evidence of how unhappy she was. I also could have focused on all of the other self-love lessons in my life – the ones that told me that I was entirely lovable.

Isn't this one of the most irritating things about being a human? We always find it SO much easier to remember and obsess over the negative rather than the positive. Take a moment to do this mini experiment – think of something that happened recently that really hurt you. Now think of an incident when somebody praised you. Which of these have you spent the most time and energy dwelling upon? If it's the praise, then congratulations, that's fantastic, but my bet is that you've focused way more time and energy on the hurt. When it comes to our love for ourselves, it's vital that we identify the ways in which we focused on the negative lessons in our lives and start choosing positive alternatives. Sometimes, even a chance remark by a teacher, boss, friend or acquaintance can lead you to question your self-worth.

When primary school teacher Helen was eight, her

family moved to a new town. The road they moved to was a cul-de-sac with a large green in the centre. This green was a perfect place to play and formed a natural focal point for all of the kids in the street.

'When we first moved there, I thought it was great,' Helen says. 'It was like I had a ready-made group of friends right on my doorstep and it made moving to a brand-new area a lot easier. But then a couple of the older girls from the street started picking on me. It wasn't anything major and it never got physical, but it had a real drip-drip effect over the years. They would call me names like "Four Eyes" because I wore glasses and "Saddo" because I was quieter and more bookish than the other kids. I can remember getting to a point where I could barely look in the mirror because I hated myself and the way I looked – and all because of their constant abuse.'

Although Helen describes what happened to her as 'nothing major', I would disagree. Anything that makes you hate yourself like this is most definitely major and it needs to be undone. When I asked Helen how she could relearn the lesson and choose to see herself as lovable, she had what she described as a real lightbulb moment.

'I could choose to see myself as lovable by focusing on how strong I was to put up with what I did,' she replied. 'Even though it made me feel really rubbish at the time, I can hold my head up high now because I know I've never treated another person the way they treated me. I am lovable because I'm caring and kind and strong.'

After I recently wrote a post about dating on my Dare to Dream blog, I received this email from Casey:

> I'm nineteen and, one by one, my friends are all starting to couple off. I'd really like to meet someone too and I've thought about joining a dating site but something keeps stopping me. I'm afraid that my profile will seem really boring and I won't get any approaches and that would just be way too shameful!

I asked her why she thought this might happen and her reply was very telling. 'I just don't think I'm very interesting to men.' Instantly my False Love Lesson radar started bleeping like crazy. Why didn't Casey think she was interesting to men? What had caused her to believe this? We did a bit of digging and it turns out that the seed was planted back when Casey was thirteen years old.

'It was my best friend's birthday and a big group of us had gone down to the beach near where we live,' she wrote. 'Over the course of the night it became obvious that each of my friends was fancied by at least one of the boys there but none of the boys were interested in me. I sat there with a big smile on my face as I watched them all flirting with each other but in my head all I could hear was: "No one likes you, you're too boring." It was horrible.'

From that moment on, 'I'm too boring' became Casey's false love lesson – and self-fulfilling prophecy. At school she became convinced that none of the boys would ever like her so she didn't even try building friendships with them. And whenever she went out with her friends, she wore the expectation of not being 'interesting enough' to boys like a cloak of invisibility. Every time she wasn't noticed by a guy, she used it as yet another example of how boring and unlovable she was.

The only way to escape from this loop of negative self-talk is to start to question it. It was clear from Casey's emails that she had loads of female friends, so I asked her how this was possible if she really was a boring as she believed.

'Oh, they don't find me boring,' she wrote back. I asked her why. She sent me a list of reasons. 'I make them all laugh. I'm a good listener and they always say I give great advice. I'm caring. We have great chats about life.'

So why can't you be all of those things when it comes to boys? I shot back. She sent me a red-faced emoticon and a promise that she would work on relearning her self-love lesson – this time teaching herself that she was entirely lovable – and not in the least bit boring!

Your self-love lessons

Now it's over to you. It could be that reading this chapter has made you think of incidents in your own life where you've chosen to learn that you aren't lovable. Let's work together at unlearning these lessons. Take a fresh sheet of paper (a single sheet, not a page in your journal this time) and write the heading **False Love Lessons**. Under it, write a list of anything that has happened to you that has led you to believe that you're not lovable. Use the following prompts to help you:

Sometimes I lose my confidence when it comes to love because . . .

Sometimes I doubt myself when it comes to love because . . .

Sometimes I feel that I'm not lovable because . . .

How have other people made you question your self-worth? In what ways do you question your self-worth? If you find writing about any of these things painful – and I know I did! – pause for a moment and do this quick (and mighty powerful) relaxation technique:

True Face Meditation

Sit in a comfortable, upright position and close your eyes. Take a deep breath, in through the nose and out through the mouth, and tell yourself that it's perfectly okay to feel the way you do. Whether you're feeling angry or upset or hurt or scared – it's okay, it's just a feeling. Don't fight it – allow yourself to feel it. Keep breathing slowly and relaxing your body.

When you stop fighting a feeling and just allow it to be, it loses its power and starts to melt away. Visualise the feeling melting through your body now, as you keep breathing slowly and deeply. Within a few seconds of doing this, the feeling should have passed through you. Keep breathing slowly and relaxing your body until it does. Then return to the exercise.

Once you have your completed list of False Love Lessons, go through each one and see how it can be reinterpreted. Just as I reinterpreted my mum moving out by looking at all of the evidence and realising that what happened was a symptom of my parents' marriage rather than anything to do with me, find alternative meanings for your own lessons. If a cutting remark by a friend or acquaintance has made you doubt yourself, just like happened to Helen, ask yourself why that person needed to say what they did. If they were truly happy would they have said it? If they hadn't said it to you, would they have said it to someone else? Are they the type of person to pick on people generally? Did they pick on other people as well as you that time? Is there evidence that what they said says way more about them than you?

In your journal this time, create a list titled,

True Self-Love Lessons and write out these positive alternatives. Then start adding more examples of how you are lovable. List the people who clearly love you. Add things that you have said or done that have helped others in some way – kind things, loving things. Use the lists that you compiled for the exercises in Part One of this book, such as your Star Qualities and your Warrior Wisdom, to keep on adding, until you end up with a long list of all the ways in which you are truly lovable. Read it. Re-read it. Really let the truth sink in, until your only belief when it comes to self-love is this: *I am lovable*.

Flush away the rubbish

Now for a fun one. I want you to take your list of **False Self-Love Lessons** and tear it up into tiny pieces and flush it down the toilet. Enjoy the act of getting rid of this tiresome baggage. Visualise all of the mistaken beliefs about yourself that you've been carrying around, swirling off to some murky old sewer where they belong. By releasing your false beliefs, you are making way for the truth. Your truth.

I love you

The chances are, this next exercise will have you cringing or laughing or both. That's okay, as long as you do it, it's all good. Sit or stand in front of a mirror and start saying 'I love you' out loud to your reflection. Keep on saying it until you break through the barrier of self-consciousness and start saying it with meaning. If you can't say it with meaning at first, that's okay too, just keep on saying it until you do – and you will! Repeat this exercise for one minute, twice a day (preferably first thing and last thing) for at least a week. You'll be amazed at how powerful the transformation can be.

Take yourself on a date

In the next few days, arrange to take yourself on 'a date'. Just you, by yourself, somewhere you would love to go. Take yourself to the cinema when everyone else is at work. Take yourself for a long walk, somewhere scenic. Take yourself to a museum, art gallery, exhibition or vintage market. Buy yourself a treat while you're there. Spoil yourself. Be thoughtful and imaginative with yourself. Be kind and caring to yourself. Dress well for yourself. Make an effort for yourself. Because, as the well-known promotional saying goes, you're worth it. And you are – completely worth it!

Write yourself a love letter

This is another one that might make you cringe at first but don't worry – you can write your way through any embarrassment. On a fresh page in your True Face journal, write:

Dear *insert your name*,

Then write a letter to yourself, full of love (use your list of True Self-Love Lessons to help you if you like). Recount events that you've been through, things that you've done and aspects of yourself that you love. Tell yourself how proud you are. Spell it out in black and white. Really take your time and get it all down on to the page. Don't get hung up on sentence structure or grammar, just let your feelings pour out freely. Treasure this letter. Re-read it when you're having a self-love wobble. Remind yourself that you are infinitely worthy of love.

The fact is, it's only when we can say 'I love you' openly and honestly to our true selves that we are ready to say it openly and honestly to others. And the others who we say it to will be worthy of our love, because when you love yourself, *truly* love yourself, you no longer settle for second best when it comes to loving others.

If you don't love your true self, you won't live your best life **#TrueFace**

7

TRUE ROMANTIC LOVE

----------- ♥ -----------

Too many women throw themselves into romance because they're afraid of being single, then start making compromises and losing their identity. I won't do that.

Julie Delpy

How many songs or films can you name with the word 'love' in the title? How many times do you see or hear or think the word love in an average day? When you scanned the contents of this book, were you tempted to skip straight to this chapter because it was called True Romantic Love? (If so, don't worry, you are definitely not the only one!) The bottom line is, we are all slightly obsessed with romantic love. And so we should be. In its healthiest, most natural state, romantic love is the ultimate. Romantic love has the power to make the world glow, hearts sing and people dance.

It can also be totally crap – if you get it wrong. And we humans have a habit of getting romantic love wrong quite a lot – just listen to any Adele song. But why is this? Why is something that can and should be the most wonderful thing in the world also capable of being the most painful?

The short answer to that question is fear. As well as making us excited and ecstatic and alive, love can also make us feel terrified, and as we've already established, as soon as we feel frightened, our first instinct is to cover our True Face and hide behind masks. And when we hide behind masks, our relationships are DOOMED with a capital everything. How can a relationship work if you're pretending to be someone you're not, or hiding your true self behind some kind of act? You'll spend your whole time feeling intensely uncomfortable and the person you're with won't like *you*. He or she will like the someone you're pretending to be.

The Valentine's Day Meltdown

- -

I have a very good friend called Paul. He's handsome and funny and kind and always remembers my birthday. In boy terms, this makes him worth his weight in Belgian chocolate. He recently arranged to meet a woman he'd met on an online dating site. It was his first nervous foray into the world of online dating, so he'd come to me for some moral support beforehand.

When he told me about the girl he'd arranged to meet, I thought she sounded lovely – and perfect for him. She was into all the same things, her profile was well-written and light-hearted and she looked like a lot of fun. And when Paul texted me the day after his date he was so happy with how it went, he used a grand total of three smiley-face emoticons. To give this some perspective, Paul never uses smiley-face emoticons, not even the time his five-a-side team won six-nil. The date had been a night of soft-focus, straight-from-a-rom-com perfection. They had instantly hit it off, and the conversation had flowed the entire time, as had the laughter.

Fast-forward a couple of weeks. Paul and his date had now seen each other three times. Each time had built on the last; more laughter, more good conversations, some intimacy. And then came 'The Valentine's Day Meltdown'. As the name would suggest, Valentine's Day was looming and Paul was planning something special for his date. He was ready to take things to the next level; to take that one small step for mankind, yet *giant leap* for man, and transition their status from 'seeing each other' to 'boyfriend and girlfriend'. He wanted their Valentine's Day to be a surprise so, whenever his date had mentioned it, he'd been deliberately low-key. Then, the day before Valentine's Day, he received a text from her.

can we chat about tomo? xxx it read.

sure – just on my way home from work will ring when I get there xxx he replied.

ok spk soon xxx

So far so good.

Then Paul boarded a train on the London Underground and stepped straight into every commuter's worst nightmare – the train broke down, and he ended up stuck in a tunnel with no mobile signal, for nearly two hours. A journey that should have taken thirty minutes ended up taking five times as long. Paul finally got home, stressed and fed up. This wasn't helped any when he looked at his phone. Six new text messages – all from his date.

home yet? Xx, the first one read, sent twenty minutes after they'd last texted.

I really need to talk. Call me as soon as you can x, the next one read, sent ten minutes later.

ok clearly something better's come up. Let me know when ur free, came ten minutes after that (note the pointed lack of kisses).

are you with someone? sent twenty minutes later.

if u don't want to see me any more u might at least have the decency to let me know! fifteen minutes later.

And finally:

Fine. I get the message. Have a nice life!

Paul rang me in a state of shock. 'She seemed so lovely and laidback,' he wailed, 'why's she gone crazy?'

Now, I don't know the woman Paul dated – after

The Valentine's Day Meltdown he never saw her again – but I'm willing to bet that the reason for her spiral into Crazydom was that good old F-word again – fear. She was clearly already a little tense over his seeming lack of interest in celebrating Valentine's Day. Then, when he didn't call her when he said he would, her first instinct was to hit the panic button. Rather than assuming that something totally normal had happened – like him being trapped underground on an overcrowded train with a fellow commuter's stinky armpit in his face – her fear made her think the worst. And how fearful must she have been to think that in the space of a couple of hours, Paul had actually run off with someone else? The speed at which she jumped to that conclusion would definitely indicate that this woman had been badly hurt in the past. Maybe she'd been cheated on before. And maybe this led her to believe that everyone cheats – or is capable of it – and this is why she lost the plot with Paul. The real tragedy is that I'm sure the fun-loving person she was on their first few dates was her True Face. What she was showing in those texts was most definitely a Fear Face.

Just as we learn self-love lessons as we're growing up, we also learn romantic-love lessons. These can come from our own personal experiences or from the romantic experiences of those close to us, such as our parents. If these lessons are positive and inspiring and fill us with hope romantically – and we have healthy levels of self-love – we're off to a great start. If, however, our initial romantic-love lessons are negative in some way, such as a parent or partner cheating, this can have a very damaging effect.

Textual tension

- -

I know that what happened to Paul is quite an extreme example, but who hasn't acted a little crazily out of fear when it comes to their romantic lives? I know I have.

Picture the scene. Several years ago I started dating a lovely guy. He was (and still is – don't worry, I didn't kill him) talented, caring and a musician. He was (and still is, don't worry, I didn't maim him!) also extremely handsome. Because he's a musician, he's on Twitter and one of his followers was a woman I'll call @BlatantBetty. @BlatantBetty made it blatantly obvious that she adored this guy – constantly tweeting gushing praise about him and his work – which he constantly retweeted. To put it bluntly, this started really annoying me.

Then, one night, I had my own mini-meltdown. @BlatantBetty had tweeted (and he had retweeted) that she loved this guy's music sooooo much, she wanted to marry him. She referred to him as her 'husband in spirit'. Instantly, my hackles were raised. Where did she get off talking like that when she knew he was unavailable? And where did he get off, retweeting it when he knew I'd see?

But I wasn't just angry. I was afraid. I'd started to have quite strong feelings for this guy. What if this woman bulldozed her way between us with her blatant tweets? What if he became seduced by the constant flattery? The fact that he kept on retweeting it showed that he was enjoying the attention.

Now, if I had managed to stay in a True Face state of mind, I would have brushed off her comments like an irritating gnat. I would have trusted that I was quite good enough, lovable enough, *enough* enough to not feel threatened by this kind of thing. But unfortunately, I failed. And one of the reasons I failed was because of my previous partner who'd cheated on me. Subconsciously, I'd taken what had happened to me in one relationship and turned it into the massive generalisation that all men were cheats.

And this, combined with my childhood belief that I wasn't lovable – *and* a chronic case of over-tiredness – led to my own mini-meltdown.

The first text I sent him was terse, something like: what's going on with you and @BlatantBetty? His reply did nothing to placate me because the next text I sent went nuclear, accusing him of disrespecting me and not being nearly as kind and loving as he liked to make out, yada, yada, yada.

Looking back now, I think I was right to get annoyed about what was going on – I do think it is disrespectful of a guy to retweet another woman's flirty remarks – but I really regret letting fear send me so far off-kilter. My True Face is not to send crazy texts – I don't think anyone's is. The fact is, our True Faces aren't possessive or clingy or jealous – they are loving and dignified and wise. That day, though, my Fear Face took over and all dignity went sailing out of the window.

Crazy in love

- -

There's a famous saying that goes: 'The only things certain in life are death and taxes.' I'd like to make an addition to that quote because I don't think it's quite correct. As far as I'm concerned, the only things certain in life are death, taxes *and acting crazy in love*. Beyoncé wasn't kidding when she sang the song. There is scientific evidence that we all go a little nuts when we fall for someone. Take a look at what happens to our brain when we start developing feelings for someone:

Firstly, the frontal cortex shuts down. The frontal cortex is the part of our brain that controls our judgement so when it shuts down, we lose all ability to judge situations rationally. Secondly, the part of our brain that controls fear also decides to take a break. Thirdly, our body is flooded with a brain chemical called dopamine – the body's version of cocaine. This causes us to experience intense highs but it also causes a loss in appetite and makes us feel jittery. So, to summarise, the minute we start falling in love we become fearless, high as a kite, jittery, unable to eat and have no judgement. Is it any wonder we mess up?! So, if you find yourself sending a bonkers text or saying or doing something you regret, don't beat yourself up. Simply learn the lesson and move on.

Your romantic-love lessons

Take a moment to think of your own romantic-love lessons. What have your parents' or ex-partners taught you about relationships and love? I don't mean what they've *told* you. I mean what they've *shown* you, through their own example. What lessons have you subconsciously absorbed? Try using the following writing prompts in your journal to unearth them:

When it comes to romantic love I think that . . .

The thing that scares me the most about romantic relationships is . . .

My parents' relationship shows me . . .

I believe that marriage is . . .

When I think about falling in love I feel . . .

When you read back over your answers are you hearing an Inner Voice of Love speaking or is it an Inner Voice of Doom? Are the lessons you've learnt about romantic love mainly positive or negative?

If they're mainly negative, we have some work to do.

Identify your Inner Voice of Dating Doom

Write a list of all of the negative beliefs you've developed about romantic love. Just as we did in the previous chapter with your self-love lessons, we're now going to look at ways in which these statements of doom simply aren't true. Let me use my own example to demonstrate.

As I mentioned before, when I was in my early twenties, a partner cheated on me. Over the period of time that it happened, I subconsciously adopted the false belief that any guy I got involved with would probably also cheat on me. Fast-forward to my next serious relationship, with a lovely, kind-hearted guy who, it turns out, was chronically allergic to cheating. For the first year or so that we were together, my Inner Voice of Dating Doom had an absolute field day. Despite all evidence to the contrary, it would taunt me by going off on a downward spiral which went something like this:

He's going to cheat on you.

He's going to cheat on you because he's an actor.

It's a well-known fact that all actors sleep with fellow cast members on a production.

He's going to cheat on you while he's away on tour.

He's going to cheat on you because other women throw themselves at him.

He will cheat on you because your ex cheated on you.

Thankfully, this guy is from Liverpool – and people from Liverpool are made of stern stuff. They also have a brilliant sense of humour. This all stood him in great stead when it came to the early days of our relationship because it meant that he was strong enough and funny enough and out-and-out lovely enough to put up with my initial neuroses and help me relearn my lesson on romantic love. Now, when it comes to cheating, this is what I believe:

Some people cheat. Most people don't. It doesn't really matter.

All that matters is that I love and respect myself.

If a partner were to cheat on me, then it was never really meant to be. Because I – and we all – deserve true love, honesty and respect.

Find your Inner Voice of Love

- -

Now do the same for each of your negative statements about love. If your Inner Voice of Dating Doom likes to say things like:

When I think about falling in love, I feel really scared because I know I'll end up getting hurt,

take a moment to question it:

How do you know you'll end up getting hurt?

Do you know anyone who has had a positive experience of love?

Why shouldn't it be the same for you?

How do your friends see you?

Why should a romantic partner see you any differently?

Then rewrite each negative statement in a more positive, loving way, under the title, **My Inner Voice of Love.**
   For example:

When I think about falling in love, I feel so excited and happy.

Create a Romantic-Love Word Collage

Now I want you to create a Romantic-Love Word Collage. This is simply a collection of all the positive words or phrases that you associate with or want from romantic love. Make your collage as full and as optimistic as possible. If you like, use different coloured pencils or pens for each of the words to make them stand out. Here is mine to help you.

These are some of the positive words I've come to associate with and want from romantic love:

closeness, *compassion*, **friendship**, *warmth, fun,* **dates**, *kisses, hugs,* **cuddles**, *confidant, connection,* **passion**, *excitement, energy,* **heart**, *tingles, surprise,* **conversation**, *laughter, tickles,* **snug**, *cosy, strength,* **insight**, *holding-hands, arm-in-arm,* **walks**, *gifts,* notes, **poetry**, *songs, dinner,* **candlelight**, *movies,* messages, **stolen looks**, *cheeky glances, shared* moments, **treasured memories**, *perfume, aftershave,* **loving gestures**, *intimate silences, infectious giggles,* **star-gazing**, *joy, bliss,* **happiness**

By exposing the untruths our Inner Voice of Dating Doom likes to tell us, we are able to get clear on what we really want and deserve from romantic love. This in turn gives us the strength and wisdom to approach dating with our True Face on, and this is a very cool way to be – as we are about to find out . . .

When I love myself I allow others to love me
#TrueFace

8
THE TRUE FACE GUIDE TO DATING

----------- ♥ -----------

Dating is really hard because everyone puts on a front. It's really difficult to see who is who, so it is important to be yourself.

Brooke Burke

How many times have you heard or read about people finding love when 'they least expected it'? One of my closest friends was single for a grand total of five years when she was in her early twenties. For most of those five years, she would have described herself as 'looking for love'. She went on blind dates, online dates and speed dates. She had makeovers, sat on her own in coffee shops trying to look alluring and she took magazine quizzes to identify her perfect guy. When it came to looking for love, this girl was a true seeker.

Finally, after one dating disaster too many she officially gave up. She didn't just say she was giving up, while still secretly hoping Mr Right would appear, she genuinely meant it. She threw herself into pursuing various passions of hers – taking a dance class, learning how to speak Spanish, booking regular trips away. She filled her life with interesting things and people and events. And then, just when she least expected it (when she was make-up free and caked in mud on a hiking holiday) she met a guy called Tony and they fell in love. On their first date, they got to talking about what had first attracted them to each other.

'He said he really liked the way I was so natural and relaxed and that it made me a lot of fun to be around,' she told me with a bemused grin, 'even though I looked terrible.'

My friend thought she looked 'terrible' because she had no make-up on and was rocking 'extreme hiking couture'. But the fact was, Tony didn't even notice her beige thermal socks, her padded waterproof trousers or her make-up-free face – he was far too dazzled by her True Face.

We'll talk more on physical appearance later, but this is a vitally important truth when it comes to dating: your true self is far more attractive than any so-called 'cool' self you're capable of creating. My friend had such a powerful effect upon Tony because she was having fun, living life to the full and being genuine. When she gave up trying to find a man, she gave up putting on any kind of act. She gave up stressing out about how she looked or censoring what she said or did. And as a result she became a lot more relaxed. She came across to Tony as 'natural' and 'fun to be around' because that's exactly what she is – and what we all are when we stop faking it.

Why do we fake it when it comes to love?

In our society, a ridiculous amount of pressure is placed upon people to be part of a couple. It's as if the media have an obsession with us going through life, two-by-two, Noah's Ark stylie. Things are definitely improving, for sure; in previous generations women would be called 'spinsters' and 'on the shelf' if they weren't married off by the time they were twenty-two. Today, in the UK, there are almost twice as many one-person households as traditional family homes. The largest group of these 'singleton householders', as they're referred to by marketing types, are young people, aged eighteen to late twenties. While it's great that statistics like these show that it's no longer freakishly weird to be single, our attitudes need to do a bit of catching up.

At the time of writing this, I have been utterly and blissfully single for an entire year. I feel no shame in this; in fact, it's completely the opposite. I feel infinitely proud that I am strong enough and free-spirited enough to love the adventure that single life brings. But when I was younger, I definitely wouldn't have been able to say this. The brief periods of time that I was single in my twenties were fraught with fear. Fear that I would be 'on my own' for ever. Fear that no one else would ever find me attractive. And my singleton status didn't do anything to help my favourite fear back then: that I wasn't lovable.

The trouble with all this fear when it comes to dating is that it can leave you feeling kind of desperate. And not only is desperation a deeply unattractive quality, it can also make you do stupid things – like settling for second best or pretending to be someone you're not.

If I could only make myself funnier, or sexier or cooler, we tell ourselves, *then maybe someone would like me...* And on come the masks. Let's take a moment to look at these masks in more detail.

The I'm So Zany mask

Fear that we somehow aren't good enough to date can cause us to overcompensate in a big way. Stephanie is a med student, two years into her degree. Among her friends, she's known for being the loudest, craziest, most game for a laugh. She is incredibly popular and invited to every party going but, beneath her mask, she's actually deeply unhappy.

'I'd love to have a life like my best friend Cassie's,'

she confided in me. 'It's so calm and chilled compared to mine.'

Stephanie's friend Cassie is also studying medicine. She's been in a serious relationship with a Politics student called Tom since they met in the first year in Halls. In contrast, Stephanie has never had a boyfriend, 'Just a couple of disastrous drunken snogs in the Student Union Bar. I thought that by making myself the life and soul of the party I'd attract boys, but actually I think it puts them off,' she explains. 'They all want to be my friend but none of them want anything to do with me romantically.' Stephanie's True Face resolution is to try and tone down her *I'm So Zany* Mask and let her quieter true self shine through.

The I'm So Cool mask

When I started dating, I was all about playing it cool. I wore an air of indifference like a perfume – *Eau de 'Whatever!'* – and I would rather have run down the road naked singing the National Anthem than tell a boy I liked him. Of course, inside I wasn't playing it cool at all. Inside I was falling in love and having my heart broken on repeat. But on the surface you wouldn't have known that I was feeling a thing. I acted cooler than an ice-pop in Iceland.

Sometimes, when our Inner Voice of Dating Doom is telling us things like: *Love hurts! Love leaves!* Or *Love sucks!* it's all too tempting to create a seemingly impenetrable mask of cool. But it's only ever a mask. It's never how we truly feel – not deep down. And it can't stop us from getting hurt. The most it can do is stop us from *showing* that we've been hurt.

In order to remove this mask, we need to work hard at unravelling the untruths that put it there in the first place. And we need to replace our Inner Voice of Dating Doom with an inner voice of love and courage. It's so much more fun when you can just relax and be yourself with a guy, rather than constantly keep your feelings under wraps. Also, if you play it too cool, they won't even realise that you like them!

The I'm So Sexy mask

This mask has become ever more popular in recent years. The fact is, 'sexy' is everywhere. It's in our adverts, our music videos, our magazines and online. A lot of female celebrities now use sexy to promote their images, products and careers. They appear next-to-naked in music videos, simulating sex with everything from furniture to foam fingers. They say it's empowering. They do it to shock. They shock to get attention. And they want attention in order to sell more records and make more money. But we're not here to talk about them. We're here to talk about you.

Being sexy *is* empowering. It is every woman's right – if that woman is being sexy in a way that truly feels comfortable for her and it doesn't leave her feeling vulnerable and exposed. When a pop star gets naked in a video she has layers of protection that other girls don't have. Firstly – or hopefully – she will have full creative control over what gets shown. She will be the one picking the G-string, directing the crotch shot, choreographing the twerk. She will also almost certainly live in a gated mansion with a team of security guards to protect her around the clock from the unwanted attentions of a Johnny SexPest. Non-famous women or girls don't have that level of control or protection. This isn't about making judgements. It's about getting real.

The reality is that often, women and girls act sexy because they think it's what they *ought* to do, rather than what they truly want to do. But when we put on an *I'm So Sexy* mask to cover up our true self we can end up getting massively hurt. The current trend for sexting is a perfect case in point. A recent poll carried out by MTV found that one third of the fourteen- to twenty-four-year-olds they surveyed had either sent or received naked pictures via text or email. And 61 per cent of those who said they'd sent a naked picture of themselves felt pressured to do so. In the US recently there have been two cases of girls committing suicide after naked pictures that they'd sent to their boyfriends ended up going viral.

People are actually dying because of this.

The True Face approach to being sexy is quite simple. If it makes you feel uneasy, uncertain, vulnerable, scared, or bad about yourself in any way, it's not coming from your true self, so don't do it. Rihanna is one of the most overtly sexual pop stars on the planet and yet when some personal, naked photos of her were leaked to the press she described it as 'the worst thing that could ever happen to me . . . now there's nothing they don't know about me and my private life'.

Your body and your sexuality are among your most treasured gifts. If you're feeling the pressure to act sexually as a way of being as 'cool' as a certain celebrity, you need to ask yourself this question: *In my ideal world, would I really want to send this picture/*

perform this act/ dress this way? If the answer to that question is no, then ask yourself this: *Why am I even contemplating doing it?*

The True F-A-C-E dating test

- -

If a guy or girl you like is pressuring you to act in a way that makes you feel uncomfortable – or if he (or she) is acting in a way that makes you feel uncomfortable – you might need to face some uncomfortable truths. You deserve to be with someone who respects you – and your feelings. Someone who would never dream of hurting or upsetting you. You deserve to be with someone caring and understanding. Someone who likes you for you, not just for a quick sexual thrill. You deserve kindness and respect. No matter how much you like him (or her), you have to like yourself more and put your own feelings first.

Listen to your body. When you think about acting sexually in some way, how does it make you feel? If it makes you feel uptight, tense, nauseous or stressed, then pay attention to these signs. They're all your body's way of telling you that you're behaving inauthentically. Being intimate with someone should feel natural and exciting. It should make your body relax and glow. And above all, you should feel completely and utterly safe.

A really quick and easy way of telling whether a relationship is right for you is to take the True F-A-C-E test. When you're with this person, or when you're thinking about them, do they make you feel:

Free

Alive

Confident

Excited

If the answer is yes, then you know that you can be your true self with them – and that they are not hurting or stifling your true self in any way. If the answer is no, you need to get really clear on why this is, and how this can be changed. It could be that all you need to do is tell them how you're feeling. But if things still don't change, then you need to seriously think about saying no and moving on.

Protect yourself with love

Do you remember me talking about how self-love forms a protective layer around us, like a force-field? This force-field can come in really useful when it comes to the pressure to do things that make you feel uncomfortable. Go over your Self-Love Lessons from Chapter Six. Remind yourself what a wonderful person you are. Remind yourself what you are worth. Re-read your Word Collage from Chapter Seven. Remind yourself of all the things you hope and expect from love. Don't do anything that doesn't feel authentic to you. Don't do anything that isn't coming from your True Face.

Preparing for a first date

So you're going on a first date and in the days/hours/minutes beforehand your Inner Voices of Love and Doom begin a weird rap-style battle inside your head. Your Inner Voice of Love is busy coupling your first name with his surname and visualising your honeymoon, while your Inner Voice of Dating Doom has somehow acquired a loudhailer.

YOU CAN'T WEAR THAT!

YOU CAN'T SAY THAT!

YOU'RE GOING TO BORE HIM TO TEARS!

IT'S GOING TO BE SO AWKWARD/ EMBARRASSING!

HE MIGHT NOT EVEN SHOW UP!

WHAT IF HE DOESN'T SHOW UP?!

By the time you get to the actual date you're a nervous wreck. Now, all first dates are nerve-racking, but here's a quick True Face checklist to help you show up as happy and laidback as possible:

♥ Re-read your **True Face Manifesto** from Part One of this book. This is who you are. Your date is lucky to be spending time with you – there's no need to be afraid.

♥ Find your own personal True Face anthem – a song that makes you feel happy and empowered. Play it loud while you get ready for the date and let the words fire you up from the inside.

♥ Take the pressure right off yourself and your date by seeing 'the date' for exactly what it is – just two people spending some time together.

♥ Try to approach it as you would a night out with a friend.

♥ Re-read the 'Crazy in love' section from the previous chapter and know that there is a scientific reason for any weird feelings you might be experiencing.

♥ Wear something that makes you feel confident – and *comfortable*. You do not want your outfit making you feel racked with insecurity.

♥ Know that your life is a great adventure story. Some of the people you meet stay for whole chapters. Some, the entire book. And some only stay for a page. But they all add to the richness and depth of your experience.

When it all goes wrong . . . walking away with dignity

- -

Never is it more tempting to hide behind a mask than when somebody tells you they want to break up with you. You've opened up to another human being; told them you liked them; maybe even told them you love them, and then they tell you it's over. Your heart feels crushed. Your ego shattered. Being dumped is horrible, there's no quick and easy way of glossing over the pain. But, if you manage to stay True Face throughout, you can definitely minimise the heartache. Recently, my friend Lisa was quite brutally dumped and yet she handled it in such a dignified way that I asked her if I could share it with you here.

Lisa had been going out with her partner for almost three years and in that time they'd built up a relationship that seemed so happy and solid that everyone who knew them felt certain that their path to true love would end in 'I do'. But then one day, seemingly out of the blue, Lisa's partner told her that he no longer loved her and that he was leaving her for a mutual friend of theirs. It was a double blow of the bitterest kind but Lisa managed to navigate her way through the pain with her head held high. And she did this by staying true to herself and putting her own self-care at the top of her priorities. Yes, she cried oceans of tears. Yes, she got angry. Yes, she felt like, and I quote, 'going round there and making them both eat their own teeth'.

But she didn't. She kept her grief and her anger private. She didn't resort to snide comments on Facebook, she simply blocked and deleted any painful reminders of their relationship. She also embarked upon a programme of self-care which included a week away in Scotland, a pamper day at a spa and a shopping spree purely for treats. By allowing herself to work through her pain in this private and self-loving way she was able to come through it a lot quicker than if she'd succumbed to her anger and fear and put on a mask of bitterness.

Identifying your dating masks

- -

So, now it's over to you. What masks are you wearing when it comes to dating and relationships? How do you pretend to be something or someone you're not when you're trying to attract a guy? In what ways has this made you feel uncomfortable? Free-write answers to these questions in your journal and see what comes up, using the following prompts to help you:

Sometimes, when I'm trying to impress someone, I pretend that . . .

I feel uncomfortable when I wear . . .

I know I'm not being my true self when I . . .

In order to be more authentic when it comes to dating I need to stop . . .

Finish by reflecting on how you could be more *you*, when it comes to matters of the heart, using the following prompts:

From now on, I'm going to keep it real when it comes to relationships by . . .

I'll feel more confident if I wear . . .

When I'm chatting to someone I like I'll focus on

...ngths, which are . . .

Potential partners will love me for the same reasons as my friends and family do, which are . . .

There's no such thing as the 'perfect man'

Just as it's completely impossible for us to be 'perfect' so it is for our potential partners. It might be that you've built a very clear picture in your mind of the kind of person you'd like to date. We've all done the magazine quizzes. Height, hair colour, weight, fashion sense – just like a detective building an e-fit, you've built a profile of your Most Wanted and now nothing will sway you from it. Big mistake.

Instead of spending hours focusing on how you want your future partner to look, focus instead on *how you want him to make you feel.* When you are living your life from a True Face perspective, your feelings are your compass. The feelings, Free, Alive, Confident, Excited form your true north but what other feelings do you want to experience when it comes to love? Jot them down in your journal now. Hopefully, they will be things like: *happy, joyful, loved, in love.* Keep these feelings as your checklist when it comes to dating, but leave everything else (like looks, interests, height etc.) entirely open. This approach can lead to some wonderful surprises. It could be that you'd always imagined your 'perfect guy' to be a sultry Brazilian with snake-like hips, but actually, when you focus on who makes you happiest, it turns out to be a kind-hearted mountain of a man from Milton Keynes.

The bottom line is, love comes in all kinds of great packages. By taking the True F-A-C-E test and making your feelings your guide, you increase your chances of finding true love and, most importantly, you stay true to you.

When in doubt, ask: Does it make me feel: Free? Alive? Confident? Excited? **#TrueFace**

PART THREE

PART THREE

* * * * * * * *

True Life

9
TRUE BODY IMAGE

----------- ☀ -----------

*In Hollywood, I'm obese. I'm considered
a fat actress but I'm never going to starve
myself for a part. I don't want little girls to
be like, 'Oh, I want to look like Katniss so
I'm going to skip dinner.' I was trying to get
my body to look fit and strong – not thin and
underfed.*

Jennifer Lawrence

I have a memory that perfectly sums up how badly I used to treat my body. I was twenty years old and locked inside a nightclub toilet. Outside, the music was thumping. Inside, my heart was pounding. I was about to take some drugs. Then the thought crossed my mind that I didn't actually know what I was about to put inside my body. *What if it's been cut with something else? What if it makes me ill . . . or die?* I stood there for a moment, wondering if I should just flush the white powder away. And then another thought struck me: *I don't care.*

I didn't care that what I was about to put in my body might kill me. I was prepared to take that ultimate risk for a short-term high. But this wasn't the only way I abused my body. I'd started smoking and drinking at the age of fourteen and my relationship with food could definitely be classed as 'complicated'. Thankfully, I never developed a full-on eating disorder but for many years, my eating formed a weird cycle of comfort-eating chocolate, then 'compensating' for the excess calories I'd consumed by only eating toast for dinner. If people told me I looked thin, I'd feel a winner's glow of pride. I'd fully absorbed all of the crap from the magazines I read, which said that thin = good (and anything over thin = fat, which = very bad indeed).

In a recent interview with the fashion website *Women's Wear Daily*, the supermodel Kate Moss said that she lives her life by the motto, 'Nothing tastes as good as skinny feels'. If I'd heard this back when I was on my chocolate and toast diet, I would have agreed. But now I know the truth. Now I know that even cold lumpy porridge tastes better than skinny feels – if that 'skinny' is rooted in media pressure and fear and self-loathing. If someone were to say to me now, 'Nothing tastes as good as skinny feels', I would sit them down with a slice of cheesecake and a book on self-love and say, 'Oh no? Well try this.' But it took a brush with death to get me to realise how precious our bodies really are.

Five years ago, my then-partner, Steve, was diagnosed with cancer. And not just any old cancer but, it turned out, the forest fire of cancers, melanoma, a type so aggressive that once it gets inside your body it will destroy all in its way until it eventually kills you. It entered Steve's body at the base of his brain and within a matter of weeks it had transformed my tall strong, boyfriend beyond recognition. His skin turned grey. He became hunched from weakness and pain and the weight fell off him. If somebody had said, 'Nothing tastes as good as skinny feels' right then, I probably would have punched them! Steve had surgery to remove the tumour but, although the operation was a success, the doctors had nothing positive to say. 'You have about two months to live,' they told him, 'a year at the most.' That day was the first time I saw him cry. But this was my man from Liverpool, the one who'd been tough enough to deal with all of my baggage about being cheated on, so he wasn't about to give up that easily.

Prior to being diagnosed with cancer, it's fair to say that he'd had a pretty relaxed attitude when it came to his body. On the one hand, he regularly went running and cycling and worked out with weights but on the other, he loved to party and regularly drank and smoked. Following the doctor's death sentence, diet and lifestyle became Steve's way of fighting back. We went online and researched just about every anti-cancer diet in existence. Out went the ciggies and Cabernet Sauvignon, in came the green juices, whole grains and organic veggies. Steve had read that tumours need sugar and fat to grow, so he decided to try and starve any cancerous cells before they could take root. The battle for Steve's body was on. Instead of letting the cancer kill him, we were going to kill the cancer. Seeing Steve's bravery and the passion with which he fought for his body and his life had a profound effect upon me.

During that time it felt as if Death was lurking right outside the door, waiting to pounce on Steve and take him from me. But as well as being terrifying, this also threw everything into sharp focus. All of the wonderful things about life – the love and the adventures and opportunities it brings – seemed a million times more amazing. And all of the petty things that can clog our minds and clutter our lives faded into insignificance. One of these things was body image. For the first time in years, I didn't give a damn about my weight. So what if I gained an extra pound? At least I was still able to eat. So what if I was having a bad hair day? At least I still had hair. So what if someone was thinner or 'prettier' than me? At least I was still alive! Although I wasn't the one with the cancer diagnosis, I realised that it could just as easily have been me and this gave me a whole new appreciation for my health and my body.

The fact is, we are meant to eat well in order to be happy and full of vitality. Without our bodies, we can't live our lives – and without our best possible bodies, we can't live our best possible lives. Comfort-eating junk food, torturing ourselves on starvation diets, binge-drinking or drug-taking to create false highs, anorexia, bulimia, self-harming and smoking all wreck our bodies and our chances of happiness. They are all symptoms of pain and not our natural way of being. And yet . . .

Recent figures show that one in one hundred women in the UK has a clinically diagnosed eating disorder and over 50 per cent of women have a 'serious issue with food' that often leaves them on a permanent diet. Six out of ten women say that they cannot stand the way they look. Girls as young as seven are being treated in hospital for anorexia. *Girls as young as seven.*

Size 14 is not fat!

- -

When I started writing this book, I put an appeal on Twitter for people to get in touch with their own experiences of body image issues. A girl called Sophie contacted me and wrote really movingly about how our definition of 'fat' has become so far removed from reality.

I'm fourteen and at fourteen there are more important things to worry about than being a size

6 and having a big chest, she wrote. At my age, passing my GCSEs should be what matters to me, although I have been that person who has cried over the fact that they are a size 14, or the way I have some fat on my body. I have been the person who has cried because they are not 'perfect' and not pretty. But no girl should be crying over the way they look. How did society turn into a place where somebody who is a size 10, 12, 14 or 16 thinks that they are fat? How can this be right?

Circle of Shame

The answer to Sophie's question is that it *isn't* right. In fact, it is very, very wrong. But from a young age, girls are being fed a constant stream of images of how 'perfect' and 'pretty' they should look. From the tiny-waisted pink princesses in comics, movies and books, to the air-brushed celebrities in music videos and magazines – all impossible-to-achieve images of prettiness and perfection. And if a celebrity dares to show a more human, imperfect side? Well then they are instantly banished to the hell that is the 'Circle of Shame'. In case you've been lucky enough to escape this phenomenon, the Circle of Shame is a magazine creation, where any kind of blemish, fashion faux pas or so-called imperfection is circled in a photo. *Shame on you, celebrity, for having a zit! Shame on you for not shaving your armpits! Shame on you for having a spare ounce of flesh on your body! And shame of shames for daring to show a speck of cellulite!*

Actually, shame on *you*, magazine editors, for treating other women in this way.

Shame on *you*, for helping promote insecurity and self-loathing in women and girls.

Shame on *you*, for making fourteen-year-old girls cry because they aren't a size 6.

Shame on *you*, fashion designers, for inventing size zero and implying that woman have to fade away to literally nothing in order to be accepted.

Why don't you take your airbrushes and your snide remarks and your catalogue of 'fashion crimes' and go and hide in your own Circle of Shame so that we can get back to the important business of living our lives to the fullest?

So that we can get back to focusing on our exams and our careers and our true selves.

So that we can ban the words 'pretty' and 'perfect'

when it comes to talking about ourselves. Pretty as a concept isn't empowering. Pretty is insipid and weak and encourages self-comparison and self-loathing.

As the poet Katie Makkai so powerfully expresses in her incredible poem, 'Pretty' (available to view on YouTube) let's all strive to be 'pretty intelligent', 'pretty creative' and 'pretty amazing', but let's never strive to be merely pretty.

How can the media constantly promote the idea that being thin, having a big chest and gorgeous long hair is what makes you successful in life? (Sophie's email to me continued.) I've sat in lunch at school countless times with people drinking diet-shakes around me. Girls no older than sixteen drinking diet drinks, how can anybody let that happen? I once had a classmate tell me that she hadn't eaten for over a day because she was trying to lose weight. She was starving herself . . . Many times I've not eaten things for fear of getting fat and getting horrible looks and being bullied.

The rabbit food question

During a press conference for the movie *The Avengers*, a journalist asked the following questions to the movie's stars, Robert Downey Jr and Scarlett Johansson: 'Robert, in *Iron Man 1* and *Iron Man 2*, Tony Stark started off as a very egotistical character but now learns to fight in a team, so how did you approach this role bearing in mind the kind of maturity of the human being in the Tony Stark character and did you learn anything throughout the movies that you make? And Scarlett, for getting into shape for the Black Widow did you have any special kind of diet, any specific food?' At which point Scarlett turned to Robert and said, 'How come you get the really interesting existential question and I get the rabbit food question?'

This is one small incident but it is typical of the unfair expectations placed upon women and girls. We're encouraged and expected to be obsessed with how much we weigh and how we look, while boys and men can get on with the real adventure of living life to the full. And as a consequence, like Sophie, we can find ourselves too afraid to eat, or racked with guilt for having committed the sin of eating a piece of cake.

But this way of being is about as far away from our true self as we can possibly get. Girls are not born with eating disorders. As babies we don't point to our nappies and say, 'Does my bum look big in this?' Just like the false love lessons we looked at in Chapters Six and Seven, the perfect body image is another illusion that we've come to believe in. The good news is, if we look hard enough, we're able to see through the illusion to the truth. Sophie ends her email to me by writing:

> I wouldn't want someone to like me only for the way I looked. I think someone liking you for your personality is more important. I want to spend my time making something of myself and finding any way I can to throw what the media thinks of how I look in the bin.

Throwing it in the bin

One of the best ways to take the media's messages on body image and 'throw them in the bin' is to work on loving and appreciating your body just as it is.

It took the cancer diagnosis of a loved one to help me do this, but it doesn't have to be that drastic. Let's take a moment to really appreciate how miraculous our bodies are.

Did you know that your body sends messages to your brain, and vice versa, at speeds of up to 170 miles per hour? Did you know that your brain creates enough power to generate a 10 watt lightbulb? The hair on your head is virtually indestructible (as anyone who's had to unblock a bathroom plughole will testify!) The acid in your stomach is strong enough to dissolve metal. You have 60,000 miles of blood vessels inside of you – enough to span the globe twice. The surface area of each of your lungs is the same size as a tennis court. Your liver performs over 500 different functions to keep you healthy. Your sneezes travel at about 100 miles per hour, your coughs, a mere 60. Your nose can remember a mind-blowing 50,000 different scents. It takes only 17 muscles to smile and 43 to frown – we were built to be happy. Unlike any other creature in existence, your body is able to produce emotional tears. And, as we've already established back in Chapter Four, you are made of stardust. In summary, your body is a living, breathing, sneezing, crying miracle.

Write your body a thank you letter

A great way to move from self-loathing to self-loving when it comes to your body is to write it a thank you letter. Take the time to thank every single part of your body that you can think of. From thanking the tips of your toes for the way in which they help propel you forwards, to thanking the top of your scalp for the way in which it stops your body from over-heating. If you aren't sure what a particular part of the body does, then Google it to find out. And if you come to a part of your body that you are often self-critical of, or actively hate, take extra time to give it thanks. This can be really tough to do but can achieve amazing results.

When I was younger, I developed a phobia of dentists which meant that I refused to have a brace fitted. As a result, my top teeth are overcrowded. For many years, I hated my teeth with a passion. The media's obsession with the 'perfect Hollywood smile' left me feeling self-conscious and insecure. And as a natural laugher and joker, feeling self-conscious about my smile has been a total pain! When I did this exercise, it made me focus on the positive aspects of my teeth, namely the way in which they help me to eat. And feeling grateful about them in this way made me feel much more relaxed about my appearance.

You are what you eat

In her excellent guide to healthy living, *The Body Book*, actress Cameron Diaz talks in detail about the importance of loving your body and focuses on the theory that 'you are what you eat'. When she lived on a diet of pizza and burritos her skin was really bad and her energy levels were all over the place. Cameron has clearly spent a lot of time and effort studying the science of food and nutrition and is now much more careful about what she eats. She still enjoys chocolate and cheesy treats but she makes sure that the majority of her diet is made up of healthy food. By doing so, she is able to eat as often and as much as she likes and has bags of energy to pursue her passions of acting and surfing and generally living life to the full.

Just as we put petrol in a car to keep it moving, we put food in our bodies to keep us vibrant. Once, my friend Dave accidentally put diesel in his car instead of petrol. Within a few seconds the car went from purring along smoothly to jolting violently and then completely seizing up. A similar thing happens when we put the wrong kind of fuel in our bodies – we start seizing up. When you starve yourself, or eat mostly junk food, you feel like crap. Your energy levels crash and burn and this causes a similar slump in your emotions. It's impossible to feel energetic when you're about to pass out from hunger. It's impossible to feel happy when your blood sugar is on the floor. True Face is all about living your best, most authentic life. But you won't be able to do that if you're running on empty – or running on nothing but pizza and chocolate. No matter what the latest celebrity diet crazes say, we need protein and carbohydrates and fresh fruit and vegetables to thrive. We were not built to starve ourselves or deprive ourselves of certain major food groups. But with so many conflicting messages out there, what the hell *is* a healthy diet?

The good news is, it's actually pretty simple, and I'm making it even simpler still by splitting it into two lists: the energy-giving foods that you should eat in order to live your best life and the energy-sucking foods you should be wary of and eat in moderation.

Energy-giving foods

Fruit and vegetables

What they do: Fruit and vegetables provide us with a vital source of vitamins and minerals. These are both essential for our overall health and well-being.

   How much to have: Health experts all seem to agree that we need to eat at least five portions of fruit and veg a day.

   Energy-giving examples: Apples, bananas, broccoli, spinach, oranges, strawberries, blueberries.

Carbohydrates

What they do: Provide us with energy and fibre to aid digestion.

   How much to have: Experts say that one third of our diet should be made up of carbs, so each of your main meals should include a portion which takes up one third of your plate.

   Energy-giving examples: Potatoes and wholegrain

rice, pasta, bread (wholegrain is best because it provides maximum energy).

Protein
- -

What it does: Essential for the growth and repair of your body.

How much to have: Around one third of your dietary intake should be made up of protein so, as with carbohydrates, you should be eating a portion of protein at every main meal.

Energy-giving examples: Lean cuts of chicken and red meat, fish, yoghurt, eggs, tofu, beans, nuts and seeds.

Milk and dairy products
- -

What they do: Dairy products provide protein and calcium, which is vital for healthy bones and teeth.

How much to have: Three servings a day is the recommended rule of thumb, but many dairy products are high in fat, so try to go for the low-fat options such as skimmed or semi-skimmed milk.

Examples: Milk, feta cheese, yoghurt, fromage frais.

Fats

- -

What they do: We live in a society where fat is a dirty word but actually fats are an essential part of a healthy diet. Fatty acids play a vital role in the development and health of your brain. Fats also help your body to absorb certain vitamins.

How much to have: When it comes to fats, the key is to eat the healthy kind, and that is, unsaturated.

Energy-giving examples: vegetable oil, olive oil, avocados, oily fish such as salmon, nuts and seeds.

Sugar

- -

What it does: Sugar has also been getting a bad press recently, with many people attempting to embark upon a sugar-free diet. I say 'attempting' because it is so hard to cut sugar from your diet completely as it's lurking within so many foods. But this is because we need sugar for energy. As with fats, it's just a case of keeping our sugar levels in check and getting it from the healthiest sources.

How much to have: You derive more energy and feel better if most of your sugar consumption is naturally occurring, as in a piece of fruit, rather than added to products. So beware of so-called 'health bars' or cereals that have sugar at or near the top of their list of ingredients.

Energy-giving examples: Fresh fruit, dried fruit, fruit juices.

Energy-sucking foods

Any food or drink high in saturated fats and/or added sugar are bad for your health and will make your energy levels crash and burn. Here is a list of some of the main culprits, all of which you should eat in moderation: *Fried foods, cakes, sugary drinks, pizza, hotdogs, burgers, sweets, chocolate, crisps.*

You'll note that I've said these should be eaten in moderation. I haven't said that you shouldn't eat them at all. From my own personal experience, whenever I've tried to ban certain foods outright they immediately become even more appealing than before. To me, the thought of a life without chocolate makes me want to dive head first into a box of Milk Tray. So I don't deprive myself. I treat myself every so often, and with a small amount, and for the majority of the time I fill my body with the right kind of fuel. As a consequence, I never diet and I have bags of energy.

Exercise for enjoyment – not torture

- -

Keeping fit should be fun. It should not be torturous or a way of punishing yourself and it should definitely *not* be done as some kind of bootcamp regime to make yourself thin. If this is why you've exercised in the past, I want you to wipe the slate clean and adopt a whole new approach to fitness. From now on, keeping fit should be solely about increasing your energy and happiness levels – so that you're able to have more fun, more adventure, and live your life to the full. How can you make exercise fun? By doing the things that appeal to your True Face. Use the questions below to find out what these might be.

What physical activities did you enjoy most as a young child?

Are you happiest indoors or outdoors?

Does music inspire you to move?

Do you like being in water?

Do you love to dance?

Do you like high-tempo physical activity or do you prefer stretching slowly like a cat?

Are there any TV shows or movies involving some kind of sport or physical activity that have inspired you?

From PE hater to personal trainer

- -

My friend Julia Buckley used to hate PE lessons with a passion. 'PE at my school was all about competitive sport,' she explains, 'and I just wasn't the competitive type. Plus I wasn't any good at sports, which meant I'd spend the whole lesson getting shouted at, both by the teachers and by the other girls in the team. The first time I discovered that exercise could be fun was when the PE teacher got us to do a workout video one day. I liked it so much I went out and bought the video!' This video sparked a love of fitness that Julia's ended up building an entire career around. First as a journalist and editor for a running magazine, and now as a personal trainer and author of the best-selling book, *The Fat Burn Revolution*, she is proof that anything is possible if you find your own way of making fitness fun.

As a young child, I loved watching the TV show *Fame* and I'd spend hours inventing dance routines and bribing my poor younger siblings to be students at my pretend dance school. Four years ago, when I was looking for a new way to keep fit, I started going to a dance class. I enjoyed it so much I ended up studying dance and training to become a dance teacher. It's one of the best decisions I've ever made and has brought me so much happiness and vitality. From attending dance workshops I've made new friends from all over the world. It's the most fun I've ever had 'keeping fit' and it never feels torturous or like a chore because it is something I've always loved to do.

How about you? Do the True F-A-C-E test. Jot down a list of exercise ideas in your journal that make you feel Free, Alive, Confident and Excited at the prospect of doing them.

In praise of pubic hair

I couldn't write a chapter on True Bodies without mentioning the subject of pubic hair. In recent years, our pubic hair has become yet another way in which we are made to feel bad about ourselves. The explosion of internet porn and the trend for barely-there thongs have led us to embark upon a razor-wielding war against our intimate areas. But pubic hair is natural. It is meant to be there. It has a very important job to do – and that is to protect us from infections, just as eyelashes help prevent eye infections.

I don't know if you're familiar with the story of The Emperor's New Clothes. Basically, a vain and gullible Emperor is fooled by a couple of conmen into wearing a suit of 'invisible clothes' and ends up parading before his subjects stark naked. The whole pubic hair debate makes me think of this story. We are naturally supposed to have pubic hair and yet the Perfection Police have declared that it is unsightly and must be removed at once. So, we rush out to spend fortunes on razors and creams and tweezers and waxes and undergo incredibly painful procedures in order to remove this hair from our body. But really we've all fallen for a giant con sponsored by porn makers and thong manufacturers. There used to be a time when it was considered absolutely fine to have hair in our most intimate areas. There used to be a time when we put our health and hygiene first.

If you genuinely hate your pubic hair, if you genuinely don't mind risking infection and undergoing intense pain, then wax away. But wouldn't it be nice if the rest of us decided that enough was enough; that there are far worse things than having hair on our genitals and that we have far better things to do with our time and our money, thank you? If enough of us do it, pubes might even be considered 'perfect' again. Can you imagine?!

Step fearlessly into life

It has been five years since Steve was told he only had two months to live. He is still cancer-free. Every time I look at him, glowing with health and vitality, I am reminded of what a precious gift the human body is. Day after day, it carries us through our lives, enabling us to fall in love, achieve our dreams, meet new people, go to new places, dance with excitement, jump for joy, cry tears of sadness and laugh out loud. It protects us from sickness and defends us from harm. It deserves – and *you* deserve – to be treated with the utmost love and respect. And by doing so, you are able to step forward into life energetically and fearlessly.

Without my best possible body I can't live my best possible life **#TrueFace**

10
TRUE STYLE

----------- ☀ -----------

Style is a way to say who you are without having to speak.

Rachel Zoe

Style is one of the best forms of self-expression we have. What quicker and more powerful way to let the world know who you are and what you're about than to show it in how you look? Ah, if only it were as simple and straightforward as that, life would be wonderful – and this would be the shortest chapter in the history of book-kind. But it's not – and so this isn't.

Right from when we are little kids we are pressurised to look and dress a certain way. Go clothes shopping for a baby girl and there is a real danger you might drown in the sea of pink. Go clothes shopping for a girl aged four (yes, four) and up, and the theme starts to shift from cutesy princess to miniature sex object – still with an overriding hue of pink. Here are just some of the sexually inappropriate items of clothing for young girls I've seen recently: shoes with 3.5 inch heels for eight-year-olds. Shoes with 1.5 inch heels for six-year-olds. Crotch-revealing mini skirts. High-cut hotpants. Low-cut crop tops – sequinned, natch. Padded bikinis for seven-year-olds. T-shirts with a picture of a bikini on the front for two-year-olds. And, my personal favourite, T-shirts with FUTURE WAG printed on the front for four-year-olds.

FUTURE ASTRONAUT? FUTURE ACTOR? FUTURE DOCTOR? FUTURE DETECTIVE? FUTURE MUSICIAN? FUTURE TEACHER? FUTURE LEADER? FUTURE WRITER? No, let's just teach our little girls to aspire to be the wife and/or girlfriend of someone successful. Let's not teach them to be successful in their own right.

People actually design these clothes. People actually sit down at drawing boards and think to themselves, *I know what I'm going to do today – I'm going to design some smokin' hot hotpants and heels for a four-year-old girl. They're gonna be fabulous!* And people pay them to do so! Even worse, some people – some *parents* – actually buy their creations.

But even if you've managed to escape being dressed as a FUTURE WAG as a child, as soon as you become a teenager and are able to make your own fashion choices, these 'choices' are dictated to you in no uncertain terms. Magazines, websites and celebrities all tend to push the same kind of look.

I'm not here to join the list of people queuing up to tell you how to dress. As far as I'm concerned, if you want to skip down the street in ten-inch heels and a T-shirt proclaiming you a FUTURE WAG that's absolutely fine. The only thing that matters is that you dress as *you*, for *you*, in a way that makes you feel good about yourself and strong and empowered. Remember the True F-A-C-E test? It works just as well when it comes to clothes too. If what you wear makes you feel:

Free

Alive

Confident

Excited

that's great. But if it doesn't, read on . . .

Hell on high-heels

I recently met a friend for lunch. She was going on to a party that evening so she'd come dressed in a really tight, short skirt and skyscraper heels. As she wobbled her way out of the restaurant after our lunch, I thought the wine must have gone to her head. But she wasn't drunk, she just couldn't walk in her cripplingly high shoes. As we slowly made our way up the street, with her clinging to me like a limpet, I saw a man approaching us giving her a filthy stare. As we drew level with him, he muttered a mouthful of abuse about the way she was dressed and then he spat in her face.

It was horrific and my friend and I were both deeply upset by what happened. My first instinct (and second and third instincts) was to say, 'How dare he? How dare *anyone* insult and spit at another human being over the way they are dressed?' But it's a bit more complicated than that. The fact is, there are a lot of idiots out there who will make judgements about the way we dress and we should never let them dictate our fashion choices. But what if we don't really want to dress like that in the first place? What if the clothes we're wearing are actually causing us a great deal of discomfort? What if we're only wearing shoes that cripple us and clothes that expose us because we're feeling pressured to do so by our peers or the fashion industry? Then, we are inflicting not only physical pain upon ourselves but emotional pain too, when we have to fend off the unfair judgements and unwelcome advances of others. How can this possibly make us feel free, or alive, or confident, or excited? How is this being true to ourselves? It isn't.

Invest in earplugs

Hawwa is thirteen years old and has been home-schooled her whole life. 'Before, I never really had cause to think about who I was, or what I looked like,' she says, 'but as I got older, I started to join various groups and clubs and I started meeting new people and being faced with different situations. Then one day, a few months ago, I was at my sports club. It was Ramadan so I was fasting. The sun was out in full force and everyone around me was chugging down bottles of water as fast as they could. The girls around me were rolling up their already short shorts, exposing as much skin as possible in an attempt to cool off. And there I was, the black sheep, in my long baggy tracksuit bottoms, loose, long-sleeved top and scarf. It was as if there was a spotlight shining down on my head.

'One girl asked why I wasn't having any water. I told her I was fasting and she stared at me as if I was crazy. "Your parents aren't here," she said. "You can do what you want. Go and buy yourself a drink."

'I sat there stunned. *She thinks I'm forced to do what I do, and wear what I wear,* I thought to myself miserably. *She thinks that if my parents weren't around I wouldn't be who I am now.* It hurt me, that final realisation that people mistrusted the image of who I was. But, just a few months before this incident, I had made a promise to myself to try and become even stronger in my faith and waver at nothing. I wasn't a candle flickering in the wind, I was a person. I hoped I had enough determination to help me. I am still the proverbial sore thumb in most places I go – the baggy, long-clothed girl amidst a forest of mini skirts, make-up and bare arms and legs. But since that day, I've surrounded myself with people who believe in me and accept me for who I am.

'And I invested in earplugs. Not real ones of course. But I trained myself to block out the whispers of people trying to inject their poison into my brain. I don't need to listen to them. I used to want to know what other people thought of me. I've realised now that that is the worst thing you can do. You have to ignore them. I try not to care what other people think of me and in that way, I don't worry about it.

'If someone says something to me about the way I look, I let it wash over my head and smile. Because I wouldn't change who I am for anything. And in a way, the people who made me doubt myself, well, they're the ones who made me stronger.'

I love Hawwa's idea of investing in imaginary

earplugs to block out other people's judgements of how we dress. And I think this rule can apply whether you're wearing a burkha or a bikini. As long as it's what you truly want to wear. As long as your clothes are expressing who you truly are. As long they make you feel confident and empowered, then your personal style becomes a physical representation of your True Face.

My friend Charlotte is a wonderful example of this principle in action. As a young teenager Charlotte always had a unique sense of style but when she was in sixth form, she began to lose her confidence.

'As the stress of exams and home life started to grow, I began to feel less confident about my style and less comfortable about standing out from the crowd,' she explains. 'So I started wearing the accepted sixth-form "uniform" of jeans, trainers and hoodies. I never felt it suited me but it felt so much easier to hide away and not be the focus of attention. I had hoped that blending in would make me more confident, but it didn't. Instead I felt diminished and boring. But once you've started trying to blend in with the crowd, it's very hard to stop.'

For the next four years, Charlotte dressed a lot more cautiously. 'I worried about other girls not liking me if I stood out too much; I didn't want anyone to think I was seeking attention. So I carried on living in jeans and jumpers and T-shirts. Then, when I was twenty-one, I suddenly decided that I'd had enough of hiding away. I wanted to be myself. So I bought rainbow shoes, dragged a faux cow-print mini skirt my cousin had bought me from the back of my wardrobe and started wearing vintage hats, brooches and brightly coloured tights. It felt amazing! Since then, I've always stuck to my personal style and taste – what I like and what I think suits me – rather than following trends. I love clothes that allow me to try on different lives and live them. One day, I can pretend I'm a sixties chick heading for Carnaby Street in my printed shift dress, then the next I can be a wild, free gypsy girl in my big patchwork skirt. I like to wear beautiful clothes because truly beautiful things never stop being beautiful, however old-fashioned they may become.'

I don't know about you, but reading Charlotte's story made me want to rush out to the nearest vintage market and buy an entirely new wardrobe. This, to me, is how style should be – fun, creative, exciting, and above all, a form of true self-expression. When I first met Charlotte I was going through a phase of dressing mainly in black – grey if I was feeling exceptionally colourful! Becoming her friend and seeing the incredible creations she could make from her outfits, often on a very low budget, has inspired me to become a lot more experimental in my own wardrobe. It also reminded me of how much I used to love dressing up as a child. I have an abiding memory of accompanying my dad to the shops when I was about six years old, wearing a bridesmaid's dress, fur hat and a pair of bright pink lady's shoes! As a teenager, I frequently used to trawl second-hand stores and jumble sales for clothes to customise in my own style. Somewhere along the line, I succumbed to the same fear of not wanting to stand out that Charlotte talks about so movingly.

fear of standing out + lack of confidence = dressing to blend in

Let's now take a look at some fun ways we can overcome this fear and let our True Face become our chief stylist . . .

The True Face style challenge

To find out if the clothes you're wearing are a true expression of who you really are, try this simple test. When you wear them, how do they make you feel? If the answer to that question is: confident, happy, comfortable and at ease, then I'm willing to bet that your True Face is your chief stylist. If, however, your clothes sometimes make you feel uncomfortable, self-conscious, unhappy and/or uninspired, then the chances are you're dressing for others rather than yourself.

Finding your true style

One of the first things you can do to try and identify your own unique style is to create a vision board. Trawl magazines and the internet for pictures of clothes that truly appeal to you. Don't be dictated to by current trends, study older fashions too. Which make you light up inside? Which do you think would look great on you? Cut the images out and stick them on a board or make a collage of them. Add words too, if you like. Which words sum up how you want to look? *Elegant? Chic? Romantic? Rebellious? Interesting? Edgy? Quirky?* Use these words to help you find more images of clothes that fit them. And above all, have fun!

Vintage treasure hunt

Once you are clear on how you want to look, go on a vintage treasure hunt. If you don't live near to any vintage markets or stores, check out your local charity shops or jumble sales. Chances are, you'll find loads of things that don't float your style boat, but this makes it all the more satisfying when you do find something. I do loads of clothes shopping in second-hand stores now and the things I buy there always get way more positive comments than the high street clothes I buy. As Charlotte said, truly beautiful clothes stay beautiful for ever. Another top tip when it comes to hunting for vintage treasure is to go to second-hand stores in wealthy areas. You tend to get much better quality cast-offs here and you can often find designer label clothes for a fraction of their original retail price.

One really cheap and easy way to cultivate your own unique style is through your accessories. Even the dullest outfit can be completely transformed by a statement ring or vintage brooch, or a brightly coloured handbag.

By making your style your own, by choosing to dress in a way that makes you feel happy and confident, you aren't just expressing your True Face, you're honouring it. You're saying to the world, 'This is who I am, and I'm not afraid to show it.' Is there really any better way to be?

I dress for me! #TrueFace

11
TRUE FRIENDS

----------- ☀ -----------

The older I've gotten, the more I've realised what a true friend is. So my friendship circle has changed a bit.

Aimee Teagarden

There are few things more beautiful than a true friend. A true friend is like having your own personal guardian angel, relationship counsellor, career adviser, emotional therapist and partner-in-crime all rolled into one. Our true friends are there for us through thick and thin – and all the bits in between. They are the family we get to choose; our soul sisters and brothers. They support us in living our best possible lives and they aren't afraid to tell us when they think we might be about to mess up. They would rather risk an earful from us than see us get hurt.

My best friend is called Tina. I have known her since I was eight years old. We grew up on the same council estate and soon bonded over a mutual loathing of our lives there. We used to spend hours in each other's bedrooms, listening to music and dreaming of a world of excitement and adventure away from the grim realities of estate life. We also used to make each other laugh so hard the windows would rattle and the next-door-but-one neighbours would hear. In the thirty-plus years that we have been friends, Tina and I have been constants in each other's lives, cheering each other on through the good times – the first boyfriends, first jobs, first homes away from home, our career successes.

We have also been rocks of support for each other during the hard times; the break-ups, the losses, our lives as single parents. Like the rings inside an oak tree, with each year that passes, another layer is added to our friendship. Tina helped put me back together again after my most difficult relationship, reminding me of who I was and what I was capable of, when my sense of self was lying, broken, on the floor. She encouraged me in my fledgling writing career, reading first drafts and offering constructive feedback that spurred me on to approach literary agents. And she became my emotional safety valve when my partner was diagnosed with cancer, providing me with a shoulder to cry oceans on. Over the years, she has also provided very timely WTF?s, whenever she sees me about to make a massive mistake – usually this has been to do with men. In fact, I think it's *always* been to do with men! In short, my friendship with Tina is the longest and most enduring love story of my life.

When we are living from a True Face perspective, trying to keep it real in every aspect of our lives, it greatly increases our chances of having rich and lasting friendships like this. But friendships can sometimes be a minefield. Just as in our romantic relationships, our need to be loved and accepted can often lead to us making wrong choices and settling for second best. In this chapter, I'm going to identify some of the ways in which our friendships can go astray and help you get clear on the kind of true friend you want to have – and to be.

Beware of the Wolf in BFF clothing

In a perfect world, our friends should make us feel great about ourselves all the time, but as we all know, the world isn't perfect and sometimes friendships can get very complicated. Jealousy, insecurity or fear can cause friends to say and do things that cause us pain. And this in turn can make us question our self-worth – after all, if someone we care about says something hurtful, their words tend to stick. This is something Louisa knows about only too well.

On the surface, Louisa's life is like something straight from the pages of a glossy magazine. She works for an ultra trendy media company in an ultra trendy part of London – a place so hip even the cake shops have names like The Boho Bake. Her life is a heady blur of launch parties, press conferences and overseas trips. She looks great and has a circle of friends wider than the Grand Canyon. And yet . . .

One of Louisa's closest friends at work is a woman called Chloe. Chloe is talented, attractive and bubbly. She is also a world champion in the sinister art of the back-handed compliment. You might have heard of the saying, a wolf in sheep's clothing? Well, Chloe is a wolf in BFF clothing. Although she makes a big deal of being really great friends with Louisa, she also takes every opportunity to put Louisa down. Here are just a few examples:

One lunch break, Louisa and Chloe were poring over the latest edition of *Grazia* and Louisa expressed an interest in buying one of the cape coats featured. Chloe's response? 'Wow, that's so brave of you! I always think those kind of clothes look so much better on models.' The result: Louisa ended up never buying a cape and spending untold amounts of time stressing over whether her clothes made her look stupid.

One Friday night over a glass of Pinot, Louisa confided in Chloe that she was developing feelings for a guy named Martin who works in their marketing department. Prior to Louisa's revelation, Chloe had barely mentioned Martin. After the revelation, she barely stopped. But it wasn't to offer her friend moral support in her crush, it was to talk – in minute detail – about every nice thing Martin had said and done to *her*. The result: Louisa ended up thinking that Martin had feelings for Chloe and questioning how she could have ever thought he'd actually like her.

And another time, Louisa had worked really hard on a presentation for work, confiding in Chloe how nervous she was about it. In the end, the presentation went brilliantly. Louisa's bosses were well and truly wowed and all of her colleagues bombarded her with praise. All except Chloe, whose silence was deafening. The result: instead of soaking up the well-earned praise, Louisa wasted time and energy stressing over her friend's non-response and wondering what she'd done wrong or could have done better.

After two years of friendship with Chloe, Louisa's confidence levels had taken a definite nose-dive. The drip-drip effect of spending so much time with someone so subtly undermining was scarily powerful. Chloe's stream of passive aggressive putdowns left Louisa with the mistaken belief that she was unattractive, untalented and unlovable. It had caused her to lose sight of her true self in a fog of self-doubt. If you have been similarly affected by a wolf in BFF clothing, it doesn't have to be this way. All you need to do is examine the 'evidence' a bit more closely and get back to the truth.

When Louisa turned the focus away from herself and on to Chloe, the result was liberating. Chloe permanently struggled with her weight. She'd been through a very painful break-up. And she had twice been passed over for promotion at work. In short, Chloe was very unhappy with her own life and tried to ease that pain by bringing other people down – especially if those other people were succeeding in the areas she saw herself failing in. Chloe was envious of Louisa. That was all. As soon as Louisa realised this, she was able to let herself off the hook and get back to feeling good about herself again. And although she started to distance herself from Chloe, she was able to do so without bitterness because she was able to feel sorry for her instead.

Personally, I think a lot of the envy that can bubble up in female friendships is due to the insane pressure on us to be perfect. As we've seen in previous chapters, such a massive deal is made about the importance of looking flawless and beautiful, it's hard not to feel a stab of envy when we see someone we deem to be more attractive than us.

pressure to be perfect + fear that we aren't = potential for jealousy

The tragedy is that this envy can trickle into our friendships too, and instead of building each other up, we seek false comfort by knocking each other down. And it is false comfort because being mean to or about others never changes our own situation for the better.

Toxic gossip

- -

I once worked in a huge open-plan office full of women. Every day, as well as having a lunch break and a morning coffee break, there would be a naturally occurring 'gossip break', where one person or other would start sniping about someone and work would grind to a halt. Sometimes the gossiping would be about a celebrity but more often, it would be about someone at our workplace; about something they had said or done, or about the way they looked. Often, this person was a so-called friend of the one doing the sniping. Although a lot of us didn't join in with the gossip session, we never once called them out on it. Instead we would sit there in silence, or nod and laugh along. The fact is, gossiping can be bonding. It can make us feel superior. It can make us feel part of a friendship group – better to be with the gossip than be gossiped about. But I don't believe that being nasty is our true state. Being nasty is only ever a symptom of some deep inner sadness or insecurity or pain.

It can take a lot of courage to stay true to yourself in the face of a good old gossip session. It can take nerves of steel to say, 'Actually, I don't think what you're saying is fair or true,' and simply walk away. But wouldn't it be great if we all started saying enough is enough when it comes to gossiping? Wouldn't it be great if we all started concentrating on the more positive ways of bonding, like focusing on having fun times and supporting each other. It would be insane to expect the world to become one massive friendship group, singing in perfect harmony beneath a cloud of snow white turtle doves. But, if we genuinely don't like someone, why not keep our mouths shut about it and focus on who we do like instead?

When gossiping turns to bullying

In the world of female friendships, there can be a very thin line between gossipy remarks and outright bullying. Over the past couple of years, I've written two books about bullying and as a result, I've received many emails from readers, detailing their own heartbreaking experiences of friendships gone sour. Recently, I received this email from Charli:

I'm bookish, I'm academic and I'm a tomboy. Those three things, added to the fact that I always had spots and was a little bit tubby, made me an automatic target for the popular girls in the school. They zoned in on me, predators to prey. I had no friends to defend me and at this point my life felt fraught with danger. I already had issues at home and the bullying broke me, for a while. I hid away in the corners of the playground, reading a book. Sometimes it worked. Sometimes it didn't. It depended how fast I could hide.

In Year 4, I gained a best friend. Simran and I were unstoppable, Super Simmi and Chick Charli. Untouchable. Then, in the November of Year 5,

Simran died. I was heartbroken and alone once again. One of the bystanders of the bullying became friends with me and for a while it was okay. But then she dropped me like a hot potato when I refused to do her homework and didn't have any revision tips for the 11+ exam that was coming up. She became the ringleader and bullied me continuously. It was unbearable, but I found ways round it. Two nights a week, I started going to after-school clubs. It was probably one of the best decisions I've ever made because I'm still at both now. I think if you're being bullied you just have to try and find other places to go and be, busy yourself and have some fun. If you can't go over it or under it, you have to go through it, but with a smile on your face.

I still go to the same school as my bully and I see her around. I look happier than her now, ironically enough. Throughout all of this, I stayed myself. I always will. Still bookish, still academic, still a tomboy, still have spots. I'm achieving everything I've always wanted to and running a successful book blog. Every time I see one of the girls who bullied me, I say a silent thank you. Because they've made me what I am today.

And that is my true face.

None of us are born bullies

- -

If you've found yourself bullying other people, or if you've sat by while your friends have bullied others, re-read Charli's words and let them really sink in. Bullying isn't just an irritation, like a bad hair day or a missed bus, it actually 'breaks' people. It makes their lives something dangerous to survive rather than something incredible to enjoy. It makes them want to hide away and cry. And, in a lot of cases, it makes them want to die. Is destroying someone else's life in this way really worth any short-term high? Is this really the kind of person you are at heart? Of course it isn't. None of us are born bullies. You need to take responsibility for yourself and your actions and ask yourself what's making you behave in this way. Why do you need to put another person down? What pain inside of yourself do you need to heal? How could you go about doing this in a way that doesn't hurt others? Surely it's better to focus on caring for yourself than hating others?

Creating a bully-proof vest

If, on the other hand you, like Charli, have suffered at the hands of bullies and are despairing of ever finding a true friend, it's vital that you don't feel powerless. You might not be able to control what other people are doing to you at the moment, but you have complete control over how you choose to react.

Charli is an inspiration because she didn't let her bullies change her. She remained proud of her true self and focused on her dreams to get her through the tough times.

You can do the same using the exercises in this book. Get clear on your Star Qualities and your True Passions and this will help you identify your own dreams. Rewrite your self-love lessons so that you are crystal clear that your bully is the one with the deep-rooted problems, not you. And read your True Face Manifesto every day. Trust that you are a great person and know that this will ultimately bring you true friends.

What makes a true friend?

In my bid to get really clear on what makes a true friend I put an appeal on Facebook. The responses I got below make up a beautiful patchwork of friendship qualities. Use them to check and see if you have – and are – a true friend:

☀ Someone you can absolutely be yourself with.

☀ Someone who is there for you in bad times as well as good.

☀ Someone who won't judge you, but will tell you if they think you're making a fool of yourself.

☀ Someone who knows what you're going to say before you've even finished the sentence.

☀ Someone who understands every bit of you and loves you anyway.

☀ Someone who will offer advice if needed but won't shove it down your throat.

☀ Someone who loves every annoying, amusing, alarming, amazing bit of you.

☀ Someone who laughs with you and cries with you.

☀ Someone who is a great listener.

☀ Someone with whom you can laugh so hard it makes your face and stomach hurt.

☀ My meatballs (*this was from my friend Kemi, who makes a mean meatball!*).

☀ Someone who just knows what you need without you having to say anything.

☀ Someone who supplies endless lemon squash and biscuits while you harp on about the latest drama in your love life (*this was from my best friend, Tina!*).

☀ Someone who loves you despite your flaws and mistakes.

☀ Someone you feel instantly comfortable with, even if you haven't seen each other for ages.

☀ Someone you trust with your innermost feelings.

☀ Someone who does what they say they are going to do.

☀ Someone who accepts and appreciates your differences and your similarities.

☀ Someone who has an endless supply of chocolate!

☀ Someone who you may not always see but you know they're always there.

☀ Someone who will always forgive you.

☀ Someone who is as true to you behind your back as they are to your face.

How to be a true friend

- -

The great thing is, the more you focus on *being* all the wonderful things listed above, the more you are likely to *receive* them. Below are a couple of simple exercises, designed to help you be – and attract – a true friend.

Practise random acts of kindness

- -

Getting into the habit of being caring is a great way to attract other caring people into your life. And a really fun and simple way to do this is to start practising random acts of kindness. Every day, try to do one random nice thing for another person. It could be as simple as offering a seat to someone on a crowded bus, smiling at a stranger or sending someone a caring text. (For some heart-warming examples of this in action, check out the official Random Acts of Kindness website: www.randomactsofkindness.org.)

Create your own true friendship code

To help you get really clear on the type of friend you want to be, why not create your own friendship code in your True Face journal. Use the template below to help you:

I, [INSERT NAME] do solemnly promise that from this day forth I shall be a True Friend and nothing but a True Friend.

I shall make my friends smile by . . .

I shall make them feel good about themselves by . . .

I will not gossip about people behind their backs. Instead I will . . .

And I'll be proud of the way in which I . . .

Whenever a friend needs me I shall . . .

Once you have it down in writing it makes it a lot easier to put it into practice.

This book is all about becoming and celebrating your true self. Our true friends support us in this process – as we do them in theirs. Together we create a space to be our true selves without judgement. If you feel that you can't be your true self with a certain friend or friends, it's okay. As long as you have at least one friend to be true with that's all you need. And if right now, you don't have anybody in your life who fits the true friend bill, don't panic. One sure-fire way of finding other like-minded people is to start following your true calling. And to find out how to do that, simply turn the page . . .

Our true friends are the family we get to choose
#TrueFace

12
FINDING YOUR TRUE CALLING

----------- ☀ -----------

Let us make our future now, and let us make our dreams tomorrow's reality.

Malala Yousafzai

On Tuesday 9 October 2012, a fifteen-year-old girl was on her way home from school with her friends when some men stopped the bus they were travelling on. One of the men came to the back of the bus, where the girl was sitting, and he asked for her by name. As her friends instinctively turned to look at her, he shot her in the head. Her crime? From the age of eleven, Malala Yousafzai had been passionately campaigning for the rights of girls to have an education in Afghanistan. As part of that campaign she had written a blog for the BBC about life under the Taliban and featured in a documentary for the *New York Times*. Her bravery brought world attention to the fact that the Taliban were trying to ban girls from going to school. It also nearly cost her her life. Thankfully, Malala didn't die. She now lives in the UK and continues to follow her true calling, fearlessly campaigning for the rights of girls and women to an education. 'I raise up my voice not so I can shout,' Malala says, 'but so that those without a voice can be heard.'

On Monday 6 July 1942, a thirteen-year-old girl in Holland was forced to flee into hiding from the Nazis, living in a cramped annexe with her family and three other people for over two years. Despite living in such uncomfortable and terrifying conditions, Anne Frank focused her energy into her true calling as a writer.

'When I write I can shake off all my cares,' she wrote. 'My sorrow disappears, my spirits are revived! But, and that's a big question, will I ever be able to write something great, will I ever become a journalist or writer?'

What Anne didn't realise was that she was already a writer and her diary would go on to sell millions of copies around the globe. The tragedy was, she never got to see her success, dying in the Bergen-Belsen concentration camp just a few weeks before the end of the war.

On 28 December 1920, a twenty-three-year-old woman visited an air field in America and was given a flight in a plane that would change her life for ever. By the time she got back down to the ground Amelia Earhart knew that flying was her true calling. She started working all the hours she could, in many different jobs, from truck driver to photographer, to save up the $1,000 she needed for lessons. Once she had the money saved, she had to make the arduous journey to her lessons alone, taking a bus to the end of the line and then walking for four miles each way. On 22 October 1922, at just twenty-five years old, Amelia Earhart set the world record for the first woman to fly at an altitude of 14,000 feet. In 1932 she became the first woman to fly solo across the Atlantic.

'Fears are paper tigers,' she said at the time. 'You can do anything you decide to do. You can act to change and control your life and the procedure, the process is its own reward.'

In 1867 Maria Sklodowska (who would go on to become internationally renowned by her married name, Marie Curie) was born. At school, Marie became passionate about the sciences but she was unable to go on to university because her family were so poor she couldn't afford the fees. Undeterred, from the age of eighteen to twenty-four Marie taught herself at home and worked hard to save the necessary funds to put herself through uni. In 1893 she finally obtained a degree in Physics. In 1903 she became the first woman to win a Nobel Prize. Her ground-breaking work and discoveries revolutionised physics and led to the development of radiotherapy as a treatment and cure for cancer. 'We must have perseverance and above all, confidence in ourselves,' she wrote. 'We must believe that we are gifted for something and that this thing must be attained.'

On 27 June 1880 a healthy baby girl called Helen Keller was born in the American state of Alabama. Nineteen months later, she was struck by an illness that would leave her permanently deaf and blind. But Helen Keller's passion for knowledge meant that by the time she was twenty-two, she'd published her first book and by the time she was twenty-four, she'd become the first blind person to earn a Bachelor of Arts degree. Helen Keller went on to become a world-famous speaker and author. She was also an avid campaigner for women's right to vote. 'Life is either a great adventure or nothing,' she wrote. 'True happiness is not attained through self-gratification, but through fidelity to a worthy purpose.'

In 2005, a UK poll of 1,000 fifteen- to ninteen-year-olds found that 63 per cent considered glamour model their ideal profession and 25 per cent lap dancer (other options on the list included doctor and teacher). In 2011, a study showed that more than 70 per cent of eighteen- to twenty-five-year-old women said that they would like to become famous, with 62 per cent saying they wanted this purely for the money and 25 per cent for the attention. 34 per cent said that they'd like to achieve their fame through reality TV and 22 per cent said they'd like to achieve it by sleeping with a footballer.

All through history, women and girls have courageously fought for the right to follow their true calling. Even when society, disability, or an entire army tried to stop them, they remained true to themselves and blazed their own trail, leaving words of wisdom and inspiration for us along the way. But now, at a time when most of us have never had so much freedom or opportunity, we are being encouraged to play small, follow the herd and chase after empty dreams like 'fame' and 'celebrity'. In spite of all our advantages, in some ways, it has never been harder to follow our true calling. But it *is* possible – and hopefully reading this book and doing the exercises in each chapter has reignited your authentic dreams and passions.

Several years ago, I was asked to run a weekly writing workshop for a London council. From time to time, the council would book a special guest author to come and speak to the group. One of these guests was a woman called Preethi Nair and the story of how she came to follow her true calling as a writer was so inspiring and so downright fun that I had to share it with you here.

Preethi began her working life as a management consultant but, as an exceptionally creative person, it wasn't long before she began feeling stifled and unhappy. So every day on the train into work, she began pursuing her passion for writing. Every day, she would write a page or so of a story and after three years, she finally had a completed novel. Then, without telling her parents, who she was living with at the time, she handed her notice in at her job and started sending the novel out to literary agents. But all of the manuscripts kept being returned, rejected. At that point, it would have been really easy for Preethi to panic and ask her boss for her job back, but she didn't. Instead, she decided to get even more creative. Every day, she would put on her suit, pretend to her parents that she was going to work, and head off to the library. While at the library, she got crystal clear on what she wanted her dream career to be: an international novelist, and writer of plays and films.

Then she came up with an extremely daring and creative plan to help her achieve her dream. She set up her own self-publishing company, published her own book *and* created her own publicist to help promote the book! She named this publicist Pru, and was so effective in her alter-ego's role that she was actually shortlisted as publicist of the year. Preethi had us all in stitches as she described how she would ring up radio and TV shows pretending to be Pru, trying to book herself (as Preethi the writer) as a guest. Sometimes, if the show's producers wanted to speak with Preethi immediately, she would have to pretend to go and get herself and put on a different voice to avoid being busted! In the end, through sheer hard work, limitless imagination and shed-loads of determination, Preethi got her book into the bestseller charts and ended up with a three-book deal with HarperCollins. She is now published internationally and one of her books is being developed by the BBC into a film.

Another great example of someone who changed her life dramatically in order to follow her true calling is Beth Reacher. Beth is now a very happy and successful life coach, and founder of TheCareerStylist.com. But it hasn't always been that way. Like Preethi, for several years, Beth floundered in a career that definitely wasn't her true calling. Here she describes what happened and how she managed to find the courage to pursue her dream career.

'Looking back now, I can clearly see how my early career path was taking me further and further away from my true self. Like a lot of young women today, I left university without any clear idea of what I really wanted to do. I was so busy following the rules; getting the right academic credentials, being the young woman I should be to fit in with my peers, that I never really took the time to ask the fundamental questions: *Who am I? What lights me up? What do I want to contribute to the world?*

'I remember leaving uni and feeling really afraid. Now I was in the real world, I could no longer hide behind lectures and a string of As – I had to go out there and forge a path for myself that would make it all worthwhile.'

Beth fell into the trap that so many of us do – she let fear dictate her career choices – fear of standing out or looking different or not fitting in. So she tailored her dreams accordingly, applying for popular graduate jobs without asking herself if this was what she truly wanted to do.

'I started my career in media sales, before going on to work in the recruitment industry,' Beth explains. 'It was here that my sense of dissatisfaction and unhappiness really set in. It's hard to put a finger on it exactly, but I just knew deep in my gut that I wasn't meant to be there. Although on the outside I had a lot of the trappings of so-called success; a great salary, popularity, and the prestige of working for a good company, there was this constant unease. Things just felt wrong. The stiff corporate suit I had to wear irritated me, time went by so slowly and I felt sluggish. There was literally no one in the office who inspired me. I looked at my boss and thought *I don't want to be you* and that is always a sign that you're not on your authentic path!'

Are the feelings Beth describes here ringing any bells for you? Do you ever feel as if the life you're living doesn't quite fit you properly? Do you ever feel as if you're going through the motions on a course or in a career that doesn't really suit you? It's so easy to let fear divert you from your true calling. But the good news is, once you've realised that you've taken a wrong turning in your life, it's entirely possible to get back on track. In Beth's case, it was reading a book that made her see the light, as she explains here:

'What really changed things for me was reading a wonderful self-development book called *The Monk Who Sold his Ferrari*. In it, a miserable lawyer nearly dies of a heart attack, which makes him realise how short life is, so he goes on to change his life in amazing and inspiring ways. It really opened my eyes and made me realise that I wanted to leave this planet knowing I had given it my all and that I'd been true to myself.

'I didn't want come to the end of my life and have regrets, wishing I'd had the courage to do the things I dreamed of doing and been the woman I wanted to be. I also realised that the longer I stayed stuck on a path that wasn't true to me, the more difficult it would be to make the change in the future. So I made the decision to hand in my notice, and set up my own coaching business and online community, TheCareerStylist.com to support other women who felt like me and wanted the courage and confidence to pursue a career path that was true to them. This is so much more aligned to what inspires me and to my strengths and passions. I know now that the true me is an entrepreneur, a creator and a visionary, and now I am on my true career path, I am so much happier. I get up every day feeling motivated, and I'm proud of the work I do. Funnily enough, I've noticed that the more I am true to myself, the more success and opportunities flow my way.'

Finding your true calling

- -

Now it could be that reading these examples has left you 'all fired up with nowhere to go'. Maybe you feel really inspired by Preethi and Beth's stories but you're just not sure what your own true calling is yet. This is completely understandable. As Beth describes so well, there is an infinite amount of pressure on us to follow 'the rules' and be a part of the tribe when it comes to our life's work and this can make us lose sight of what we truly want.

pressure to fit in + fear of looking stupid = false goals

Below, I've come up with some fun and simple tests you can do to try and get clearer on your true calling. Use the list of True Passions you came up with in Chapter Two to help you and feel free to jot down your thoughts and findings in your True Face journal . . .

The Leap Out of Bed Test

As I mentioned before, once upon a time I spent two years – *two years* – working in the complaints department for a frozen food company. All day long I would have to answer irate phone calls from people who'd found all kinds of gross stuff in their ice-cream or frozen peas. They would write to me too – letters so angry they would sometimes actually write them in red, or FURIOUS CAPITALS, often containing the gross things they'd found in their frozen food, Sellotaped to the page. And let me tell you, there is nothing more stomach-churning than opening a letter to find a splattered cockroach staring up at you. So, whenever my alarm went off during those days, my first instinct was to bury my head under the pillow and pretend that I was still asleep, or, if it was Monday, dead.

However, once I began my career as a writer and life coach something really weird happened. I no longer dreaded my alarm going off. In fact, most days, I leap out of bed without even hitting the snooze button – or trying to suffocate myself with the pillow. And the reason is quite simple – I'm now lucky enough to spend my working hours doing things that I love. In short, I'm living my true calling.

Cast your mind back to the last time you couldn't wait to get up. What were you about to do? What did you have planned? Which days of the week do you look forward to the most and why? What makes you leap out of bed in the morning rather than bury your head in a pillow and wail at your alarm clock, 'Please, no!'?

The Time Flies Test

They say that time flies when you're having fun and 'they' are right! Whenever I'm writing or coaching, time zips by. But back when I worked in the Complaints Department from Frozen Food Hell, there were days when I actually thought time was going backwards. I ended up developing a completely irrational hatred for the office clock and its oh-so-slo-mo hands. And yet in the evenings and at the weekends – basically any time I wasn't in the office – time seemed to more than quadruple its speed.

Think of instances in your own life when time races by. What are you doing when that happens? What are you doing to *make* that happen? Jot down your findings in your journal now.

The Picture Test

Gather together a collection of magazines and cut out any pictures that make your heart sing. Don't over-think it; just listen to your instincts and pick out any pictures that strike a chord with you. It could be as random as a car advert or a photo of a beautifully iced cake. The rule here is – if it makes you stop and look twice – if it makes you smile – if it makes you excited or wistful or dreamy – then cut it out.

When my photographer friend, Tabitha, did this exercise, she was surprised to find herself really drawn to pictures of jewellery. Prior to that, she'd been specialising in landscape photography. Doing the Picture Test made her branch out professionally, advertising her services to jewellery designers. Not only has it made her working life way more fulfilling but it has also provided her with an additional source of income.

The 'I Wish I Had Their Job' Test

A great way of figuring out your true career calling is to ask yourself whose career you envy. Whose job do you wish you had? Or whose life do you wish you could swap with? It could be someone famous, or someone you know, it doesn't matter. If you wish you could be doing what they're doing, then write it down.

Marnie spent years studying for a law degree. 'When I was about fourteen or fifteen I remember panicking about what I was going to do with the rest of my life,' she explains. 'Law seemed like a really safe route, work-wise. And all the John Grisham novels I was reading at the time made it seem so exciting too!'

But about two years into her degree, Marnie started getting really jealous of one of her housemates, a drama student called Liz. 'Her life seemed so exciting,' Marnie says. 'She was always rehearsing for some show or another and she was part of such a fun crowd. I felt really dull by comparison as I sat poring over my books night after night. It was crazy because she was a very lovely girl but I'd find myself thinking really resentful thoughts about her. It took me ages to realise that it wasn't *her* I was resentful of, it was my choice of degree.'

Marnie finished her law degree and is now working as a trainee solicitor but she has also joined a local amateur dramatic group and is loving every minute of it. 'I'm enjoying my work as a solicitor but it's my acting that makes me feel really alive. I don't care that I'm not a professional actor – the way I see it, by being part of an am-dram group, I get to play really interesting roles virtually all the time and it's the perfect balance to my work in the office and in court.'

The Tingles Test

All the best things in life give us the tingles – that delicious, shivery sensation running up and down your spine. Anne Mortenson has spent her life listening to her body and letting it guide her in her career decisions. Whenever something gives her the tingles, she knows she's on the right path. Here, she explains why:

'I recently told my nineteen-year-old brother, who was struggling to choose a specific subject to study,

"Choose whatever you're drawn to." At his age, I wasn't clear about my direction either, so I made it my primary job to listen to my heart. What I didn't realise was, I was already well on my way to doing what I do today. My earliest ambition was to become a member of my local library. At the age of six, I urged my grandmother to register me and take me there once a week. I checked books out on everything from dinosaurs to astrology to food. I wasn't objectively aware of what I was doing at that young age but looking back now, I can see that I was in the throws of research! As I got older, I began to write, and once I was a teenager, my record-taking also took the form of photography. I would be the one at the party taking all the photos, while everyone else was talking, eating and dancing. Despite all these clues, it was only at the age of twenty that I became clear and decisive about my direction in life. I took two college classes that sealed it for me: Theory of Communication and Visual Communication. They both sent tingles up my spine. That's when I knew I was a communicator and the skills I'd honed over the years were all leading me to this path. Today, I am an award-winning art film-maker. Over the years, I've learnt that living a life that is true to yourself is all about understanding and following your heart and body's clues.'

Think about the options open to you right now. Which of them give you the tingles? Do the True F-A-C-E test. Which of them make you feel Free, Alive, Confident and Excited? What clues is your body giving you about the path in life you ought to be taking?

Achieving your true calling – one goal at a time

Once you've got clear on your true calling – so clear you can write it down in one sentence – it's time to start taking steps to make that dream a reality. Write the following headings in your journal:

My true calling

Beneath this heading write the one sentence that sums up your dream career, e.g. if you love helping others and have a strong sense of justice, you could write: '*To become a politician.*'

Five-year goals

Under this heading, write how far you would like to have come in your true calling in five years' time. It could be 'To stand for parliament' or, if you'll only just be finishing your education in five years' time, 'To have completed my Politics degree'.

One-year goals

This section is for the goals you would like to have achieved within a year, e.g. 'Do some work experience for my local MP' or 'Do well in my Politics A level'.

One-month goals

Under this title, write what steps you could take towards achieving your true calling in the next month. If your true calling is to become a politician this could be, 'Research the issues I feel most passionately about'.

This week's goals

What simple step or steps could you take in the coming week, to help you move closer to your true calling? e.g. 'Buy a book about one of the issues I feel most passionately about'.

Today's goal

What one thing could you do today, to help you achieve your longer-term goals? e.g. 'Read an interview with a politician I admire, for inspiration.'

I use this technique all the time in my own life and when I'm coaching people. I love it because it helps turn seemingly impossible-to-achieve dreams into small, easy-to-achieve steps. Try it for yourself and see.

Find a mentor

As you've seen from the examples in this chapter, the world is full of inspirational role models in every field of life. Once you've identified your true calling, or at least think you know what it might be, find a mentor in that field – they could be famous or non-famous, living or dead – and discover everything you can about how they achieved their dream. Let their courage and drive fire you up and show you that anything is possible. Move away from the air-brushed illusions of perfection and the 'famous-for-being-famous' celebrity drones and find authentic role models you can really trust: mentors who will make you feel good about yourself instead of riddled with self-doubt.

From Inner Voice of Doom to Inner Voice of Dreams

My Inner Voice of Doom shouted at its very loudest when I finally decided to follow my true calling in life and become a writer. When I started writing my first book I was twenty-seven years old and a new mum. The only time I got to write was at night when my son was asleep. Many nights I would end up hunched over my keyboard crying tears of exhaustion, as my

Inner Voice told me that I wasn't good enough and I ought to give up. But I kept on going. The pain of living a life where I wasn't being true to myself had become too great to ignore. I'd wasted years of my life in jobs that I hated and I'd ended up in a relationship that was toxic and destructive. As a result, my Inner Voice of Dreams started begging for attention. *There's got to be a better life than this*, I would say to myself. *There's got to be a happier future*. And in this way, I was able to drown out my Inner Voice of Doom and force myself to sit down at my computer and tap away, night after night until finally, my dream came true. I got my first book deal and I was able to create a new life for myself and my son. By reigniting my passion for words and books I ended up writing my way into a life of happiness, freedom and adventure; I ended up writing my way back to my true self. What does your Inner Voice of Dreams like to say to you? How is it trying to get your attention right now?

All of the women I have featured in this chapter could have succumbed to fear and ignored their true calling. Helen Keller could have allowed her disabilities to imprison her. Marie Curie could have given in to financial hardship and settled for any old job. Amelia Earhart could have seen her fears as real rather than 'paper' tigers and left the flying to the men. Anne Frank could have let her fear of Nazi capture cause her to throw her pen down in despair. And Malala could have let a Taliban bullet silence her. But all of them overcame their fears and chased after their true callings with everything they had. And in doing so, they've gifted us with an inspirational and empowering legacy.

They have shown us that the world is a far richer and more exciting place when we follow our dreams. And our lives are far happier. Don't we owe it to these women to follow our true calling and build lives that make us feel Free, Alive, Confident and Excited? Don't we owe it to *ourselves* to show our True Face to the world?

I owe it to myself to show my true face to the world
#TrueFace

CONCLUSION

------------ ★ ♥ ☀ ------------

The thing that is really hard and really amazing is giving up on being perfect and beginning the work of being yourself.

Anna Quindlen

During the process of writing this book I've learnt so much about the importance of living life from your True Face. I hope that reading it has made you feel the same way too. When you live life as your true self, everything flows more easily. Your friendships and relationships become loving and stress-free, you exude vitality and joy, and you have the sass and flair to create the life of your dreams. On the other hand, when you live life from behind a mask of fear, your relationships are inauthentic and often painful, you feel stressed and unhappy, and your Inner Voice of Doom sets up a permanent PA system inside your head.

The pressure on us to fake it in life is huge, but the rewards of keeping it real are even bigger. The way I see it, we have a choice: we can either squeeze ourselves into lives that meet the demands of the Perfection Police and shrink ourselves into carbon copies of everyone else, or we can expand into our true potential and live a life beyond our wildest, most authentic dreams.

When I'm at the end of my life, I want to look back without a trace of regret. I want to have lived wildly, loved passionately and dreamed boldly. I do not want my greatest achievement to have been that time when I starved myself into a pair of size zero jeans. I do not want *Nothing tastes as good as skinny feels* etched upon my gravestone. I want my last thought to be, *thank you*, pure and simple.

How about you . . . ?

ACKNOWLEDGEMENTS

First and foremost, I need to thank Leah Thaxton at Faber & Faber for having faith in *True Face* when it was literally just a tweet. Thank you for encouraging me to work that tweet up into an email, and that email into some sample chapters, and those sample chapters into an entire book. Thank you for sharing my passion and vision and believing in me as a writer. And to Rebecca Lewis-Oakes for being such a sensitive editor and pushing me to do my best work. And everyone else at Faber & Faber – being published by you is a dream come true. Thanks also, to my agent Erzsi Deak.

I would also like to thank everyone who has helped me find the courage to show my true face to the world: my soul sisters, Tina McKenzie, Sara Starbuck, Angela Woodward, Jenny Davies. My soul Scouser, Steve O'Toole. My coaching inspiration, Lexie Bebbington. My dance family. And my teachers – most especially, Michael Curham, for helping me see that life should be all about love and simplicity.

To everyone who has contributed to this book, thank you for sharing your experiences so honestly and passionately. To the bloggers, reviewers and readers who have been so supportive of my work, thank you so much for taking the time to contact me. Receiving your emails is one of the loveliest things about being a writer.

And last but never least, to my family: Anne, Mikey, Bea, Luke, Alice, Jack, Katie, Dan and John. Thank you so much for all of your love and support.